# DISCUSSIONS WITH TEACHERS

**[III]**

FOUNDATIONS OF WALDORF EDUCATION

# RUDOLF STEINER

# Discussions with Teachers

FIFTEEN DISCUSSIONS WITH THE TEACHERS
OF THE STUTTGART WALDORF SCHOOL
AUGUST 21–SEPTEMBER 6, 1919

THREE LECTURES ON THE CURRICULUM
SEPTEMBER 6, 1919

*&* Anthroposophic Press

*The publisher wishes to acknowledge the inspiration
and support of Connie and Robert Dulaney*

❖  ❖  ❖

Translated from shorthand reports unrevised by the lecturer from the German text: *Erziehungskunst. Seminarbesprechungen und Lehrplanvorträge.* (Vol. No. 295 in the *Bibliographical Survey*) published by Rudolf Steiner Verlag, Dornach, Switzerland, 1961. The fifteen discussions were translated by Helen Fox and revised by the publisher for this edition. English versions of the speech exercises, rendered by Maisie Jones, are from *Creative Speech: The Nature of Speech Formation*, published by Rudolf Steiner Press, London, 1978. The three lectures on the curriculum were translated by Katherine E. Creeger for this edition.

Copyright © 1997 Anthroposophic Press

Published by Anthroposophic Press
P.O. Box 749, Gt. Barrington, MA 01230

Library of Congress Cataloging-in-Publication Data

Steiner, Rudolf, 1861–1925.
    Discussions with teachers : fifteen discussions with the teachers of the Stuttgart Waldorf School from August 21 to September 6, 1919 : three lectures on the curriculum given on September 6, 1919 / Rudolf Steiner.
        p.  cm. — (Foundations of Waldorf education ; 3)
    Translations of unrevised shorthand reports that were published in 1959 as part of Erziehungskunst, Seminarbesprechungen und Lehrplanvorträge.
    Includes bibliographical references and index.
    ISBN 0-88010-408-2 (paper)
    1. Teaching.  2. Waldorf method of education.  3. Educational psychology.
I. Steiner, Rudolf, 1861–1925. Erziehungskunst, Seminarbesprechungen und Lehrplanvorträge.  II. Title.  III. Series.
LB1025.S834  1997
371.3—dc21                                                                            97-8901
                                                                                          CIP

*Printed in the United States of America*

# Contents

teenth century. Historians Buckle and Lecky recommended. Lamprecht. Freytag. H. S. Chamberlain. Socialist historians good for facts. Observing the movements of Sun and planets. Egyptian drawing. Animal-headed men. Physical strength of Egyptians; their mythology.

# Introduction

These discussions are part of the first Waldorf Teacher Training. They took place along with two other courses that Rudolf Steiner gave to prepare the individuals he had chosen as teachers for the first Waldorf school, which opened in Stuttgart on September 7, 1919.

Emil Molt, the managing director of the Waldorf-Astoria cigarette factory, had requested that Rudolf Steiner help found a school for the children of the factory employees. From that request has grown what is now a worldwide educational movement. But the questions can be asked: Is an educational impulse more than seventy-five years old relevant today? How do teachers keep themselves up-to-date? Can the Waldorf curriculum be effective for children in the twentieth and into the twenty-first centuries?

This original Waldorf teacher training was brief: it lasted only two weeks. It was understood by those who attended, however, that Waldorf education was to be based upon the continuing training or self-education of the teacher, and that this was only the beginning of that process. These fifteen discussions—along with three lectures on the curriculum, translated for the first time into English—can give the teachers of today the tools for becoming true educators.

A wealth of specific examples and commentaries is included. Suggestions for lessons, characterizations of how various stories can be brought before the children, and a perceptive knowledge of the developing human being are all available in abundant detail. However, these indications are not meant to be information that is merely copied by teacher after teacher. If they were, they would become quickly "out of date." Rudolf Steiner's training method was, instead, to elicit a lesson from the teachers themselves, and only then to make his own contribution based on what was presented. He sought the full engagement of the teacher in the subject at hand. In his closing words to these discussions, Steiner "lays upon the hearts" of the teachers to keep steadfastly to four principles:

> The teacher must be a person of initiative in everything that is done, great or small.
> The teacher should be one who is interested in the being of the whole world and of humanity.
> The teacher must be one who never makes a compromise in heart or mind with what is untrue.
> The teacher must never get stale or grow sour.[1]

Rudolf Steiner also provided steps to improve a teacher's *effectiveness*: exercises for the speech organs. These same exercises were presented earlier to members of the working group of the Threefold Social Order, who were often called upon to give lectures, and later to actors when Steiner gave the course on speech and drama in 1924.[2] Each exercise was a response to a specific need. The exercise "fulfilling goes," for instance, was first given to Emil Molt to help counteract shortness of breath. The exercises have proven themselves repeatedly over the years to be invaluable aids for training speakers. They are

---

1. Closing Words, page 181.
2. *Speech and Drama*, Anthroposophic Press, Spring Valley, NY, 1960.

included here not only for their historical interest, but primarily for their practical use. Therefore, an English version of each exercise is given in place of the original German.[3] Though it is the sound and not the sense of the exercises that matters, each language has its own organic laws. In English the rhythm and the movement of the sounds are especially important to maintain. When these exercises are practiced regularly, a teacher can develop elasticity in the speech organs. A teacher can begin to feel, for instance, how the consonants can be made to move differently depending on the neighboring vowel; and also what has to be done in order to speak a sound correctly by listening to the sound itself. This requires repetition—a hundred times during two weeks was suggested by Steiner.[4] Repetition cultivates the speech, makes it flexible, and is intimately connected with the life of the soul. Speech reveals the life of the soul. This is quintessential for the teacher.

> The inner life, the life of the soul, is the most significant aspect in the child. Teaching and education depend on what passes from the soul of the teacher to the soul of the child.... Education occurs because of what you are, or rather, let us say, what you make of yourself when you are with the children. You must never lose sight of this.[5]

---

3. The English equivalents of the German speech exercises in this edition were made by Maisie Jones and used in the London School of Speech Formation. They were first published in Rudolf Steiner and Marie Steiner-von Sivers, *Creative Speech: The Nature of Speech Formation*, Rudolf Steiner Press, London, 1978. Other English versions are also in use, notably those made by Alice Crowther, Maud Surrey, Hans Pusch, Mechthild Harkness, and Sophia Walsh. The original German exercises are included in the appendix.
4. *Creative Speech*, p.71.
5. Discussion 1, page 20.

In 1921, when Rudolf Steiner again spoke about this, he stated:

In order to start from an example, let us first take the teacher speaking to children. As far as speaking is concerned, actually the very least depends upon the genius and wisdom of the teacher. As to whether we can teach mathematics or geography well, the very, very least will depend upon whether we ourselves are good mathematicians, or good geographers. We can be outstanding geographers, but poor teachers of geography. The intrinsic worth of the teacher, which surely rests in large measure upon speaking, depends upon what the teacher has previously felt and experienced about the things to be presented, and the kinds of feelings that are again stirred up by the fact that a child is before him or her.[6]

In this book, along with its companion courses, *The Foundations of Human Experience* and *Practical Advice to Teachers,* is a foundation for the continuing self-education of teachers. These courses provide the basis out of which a teacher of today can educate a child of today, at each new moment, with a fresh and healthy mood of soul. A more modern art of education could not be created.

*Craig Giddens*

---

6. *The Art of Lecturing*, lecture one, Dornach, October 11,1921, Spring Valley, NY, Mercury Press,1984.

# Discussion One

MY DEAR FRIENDS, in these afternoon sessions I shall speak informally about your educational tasks—about the distribution of work in the school, arrangement of lessons, and so on. For the first two or three days we will have to deal mainly with the question of our relationship to the children. When we meet the children we very soon see that they have different dispositions, and despite the necessity of teaching them in classes, even large classes, we must consider their various dispositions. First, aside from everything else, we will try to become conscious of what I would say is ideal necessity. We need not be too anxious about classes being too full, because a good teacher will find the right way to handle this situation. The important thing for us to remember is the *diversity* of children and indeed of all human beings.

Such diversity can be traced to four fundamental types, and the most important task of the educator and teacher is to know and recognize these four types we call the temperaments. Even in ancient times the four basic types—the *sanguine, melancholic, phlegmatic,* and *choleric* temperaments—were differentiated. We will always find that the characteristic constitution of each child belongs to one of these classes of temperament. We must first acquire the capacity to distinguish the different types; with the help of a deeper anthroposophical understanding we must, for example, be able to distinguish clearly between the sanguine and phlegmatic types.

In spiritual science we divide the human being into *I-being, astral body, etheric body,* and *physical body.* In an ideal human being the harmony predestined by the cosmic plan would naturally predominate among these four human principles. But in reality this is not so with any individual. Thus it can be seen that the human being, when given over to the physical plane, is not yet really complete; education and teaching, however, should serve to make the human being complete. One of the four elements rules in each child, and education and teaching must harmonize these four principles.

If the I dominates—that is, if the I is already very strongly developed in a child, then we discover the melancholic temperament. It is very easy to err in this, because people sometimes view melancholic children as though they were especially favored. In reality the melancholic temperament in a child is due to the dominance of the I in the very earliest years.

If the astral body rules, we have a choleric temperament. If the etheric body dominates, we have the sanguine temperament. If the physical body dominates, we have the phlegmatic temperament.

In later life these things are connected somewhat differently, so you will find a slight variation in a lecture I once gave on the temperaments.[1] In that lecture I spoke of the temperaments in relation to the four members of the adult. With children, however, we certainly come to a proper assessment when we view the connection between temperament and the four members of the human being as I just described. This knowledge about the child should be kept in the back of our minds as we try to discover which temperament predominates through studying the whole external bearing and general habits of the child.

---

1. "The Four Temperaments" in *Anthroposophy in Everyday Life*, Anthroposophic Press, Hudson, NY, 1995.

If a child is interested in many different things, but only for a short time, quickly losing interest again, we must describe such a child as sanguine. We should make it our business to familiarize ourselves with these things so that, even when we have to deal with a great many children, we can pick out those whose interest in external impressions is quickly aroused and as quickly gone again. Such children have a sanguine temperament.

Then you should know exactly which children lean toward inner reflection and are inclined to brood over things; these are the melancholic children. It is not easy to give them impressions of the outer world. They brood quietly within themselves, but this does not mean that they are unoccupied in their inner being. On the contrary, we have the impression that they are active inwardly.

When we have the opposite impression—that children are not active inwardly and yet show no interest in the outer world, then we are dealing with the phlegmatic children.

And children who express their will strongly in a kind of blustering way are cholerics.

There are of course many other qualities through which these four types of temperament express themselves. The essential thing for us during the first few months of our teaching, however, is to observe the children, watching for these four characteristics so that we learn to recognize the four different types. In this way we can divide a class into four groups, and you should gradually rearrange the seating of the children with this goal in mind. When we have classes of boys and girls, we will have eight groups, four groups of boys and four of girls—a choleric, a sanguine, a phlegmatic, and a melancholic group.

This has a very definite purpose. Imagine that we are giving a lesson; during our teaching we will sometimes talk to the children and at other times show them things. As teachers we must be conscious that when we show something to be looked at, it is different from judging it. When we pass judgment on something we turn to one group, but when we show the children something, we turn to another. If we have something to show that should work particularly on the senses, we turn with particular attention toward the sanguine group. If we want the children to reflect on what has been shown, we turn to the melancholic children. Further details on this matter will be given later. But it is necessary to acquire the art of turning to different groups according to whether we show things or speak about them. In this way what is lacking in one group can be made good by another. Show the melancholic children something that they can express an opinion about, and show the sanguine something they can look at; these two groups will complement each other in this way. One type learns from the other; they are interested in each other, and one supplies what the other lacks.

You will have to be patient with yourselves, because this kind of treatment of children must become habit. Eventually your *feeling* must tell you which group you have to turn toward, so that you do it involuntarily, as it were. If you did it with fixed purpose you would lose your spontaneity. Thus we must come to think of this way of treating the different tendencies in the temperaments as a kind of habit in our teaching.

Now you should not hurry the preparation of your lessons, but be sure to truly strengthen yourselves for the work. I do not mean that you should spend the limited time at your disposal in a lot of detailed preparation, but nevertheless you can only make these things your own if you ponder over them in your souls. It will thus be our task to concern ourselves in a truly practical way with the *teacher's* attitude to the temperamental tendencies of children. So now we will divide the work among you as follows. I will ask one group to concern themselves with

the sanguine temperament, a second group with the phlegmatic, a third with the melancholic, and the fourth with the
choleric. And then, in our free discussions tomorrow, I would
like you to consider the following questions: first, how do you
think the child's own temperament is expressed? Second, how
should we deal with each temperament?

With regard to the second question I have something more
to say. You can see from the lecture I gave some years ago that,
when we want to help a temperament, the worst method is to
foster the opposite qualities in a child. Let's suppose we have a
sanguine child; when we try to train such a child by driving out
these qualities, we provide a bad treatment. We must work to
understand the temperament, to go out to meet it. In the case
of the sanguine child, for example, we bring as many things as
possible to the attention of the child, who becomes thoroughly
occupied, because in this way we can work with the child's pro-
pensities. The result will be that the child's connection with the
sanguine tendency will gradually weaken and the temperaments will harmonize with each other. Similarly, in the case of
the choleric child we should not try to prevent ranting and raging, but endeavor to meet the child's needs properly through
some external means. Of course it is often not so easy to allow a
child to have a fling in a fit of temper!

You will find a distinct difference between phlegmatic and
choleric children. A phlegmatic child is apathetic and is also not
very active inwardly. As teachers you must try to arouse a great
deal of sympathy within yourselves for a child of this type, and
take an interest in every sign of life in such a child; there will
always be opportunities for this. If you can only find your way
through to the apathy, the phlegmatic child can be very interesting. You should not however express this interest, but try to
appear indifferent, thus dividing your own being in two, as it
were, so that inwardly you have real sympathy, while outwardly

you act so that the child finds a reflection in you. Then you will be able to work on the child in an educational way.

With the choleric child, on the other hand, you must try to be indifferent inwardly, to look on cooly when the child is in a bad temper. For example, if the child flings a paint jar on the floor, be as phlegmatic and calm as possible outwardly during such a fit of temper—imperturbable! On the other hand, you should talk about these things with the child as much as you can, but not immediately afterward. At the time you must be as quiet as possible outwardly and say with the greatest possible calm, "Look, you threw the paint jar." The next day when the child is calm again, you should talk about the matter with the child sympathetically. Speak about what has been done and offer your sympathy and understanding. In this way you will compel the child to repeat the whole scene in memory. You should then also calmly judge what happened, how the paint jar was thrown on the floor and broke in pieces. By these means very much can be done for children who have a temper. You will not get them to master their temper in any other way.

This will guide you in dealing with the two questions we will consider tomorrow. We will arrange it so that each of you can present what you have to say. Make short notes on what you have thought of and we will talk about what you have prepared. Time must always be allowed for the teaching faculty to discuss these and similar matters. In discussions of this kind, which have a more democratic character, a substitute must be found for a dictatorial leadership like that of a headmaster, so that in reality every individual teacher can always share in the affairs and interests of the others. So tomorrow we will begin with a discussion. As a starting point I would like to give you a kind of diagram to work from.

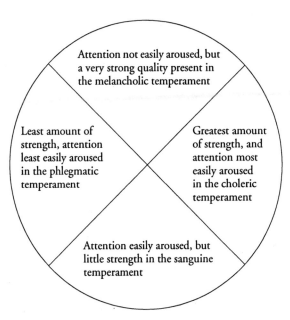

Whenever people express themselves in any way, you can tell from their dispositions whether they perceive things strongly or weakly; and further, whether they perceive and feel more strongly what is outside themselves or within their own inner situation. We must also notice whether such people are changeable or not. People either persevere at something and change very little, or show less perseverance and change greatly. This is how the various temperaments differ.

When you have observed such things you will understand certain indications about the temperaments in this diagram. Sanguine and phlegmatic temperaments are frequently found together, and you will see that they are next to each other in the diagram. You will never find a phlegmatic temperament passing easily into the choleric. They are as different as the North and South Poles. The melancholic and sanguine temperaments are also polar opposites. The temperaments that are next to each other merge into one another and mingle; so it will be good to arrange your groups as follows: if you put the phlegmatics together it is good to have the cholerics on the opposite side, and to let the two others, the melancholies and sanguines, sit between them.

All these things bring us back to what I spoke of this morning.[2] The inner life, the life of soul, is the most significant aspect in the child. Teaching and education depend on what passes from the soul of the teacher to the soul of the child.

We cannot overestimate what takes place in the hidden links that pass from one soul to another. There is, for example, a remarkable interplay between souls when you remain calm and indifferent around a choleric child, or when you have inner sympathy toward a phlegmatic child. In this way your education of the child through your own inner soul mood will have a truly supersensible quality. Education occurs because of what you are, or rather, let's say, what you make of yourself when you are with the children. You must never lose sight of this.

But children also influence each other. And that is the remarkable thing about this division into four groups of similar temperaments; when you put those that are alike together, it does not have the effect of intensifying their temperamental tendencies but of reducing them. For example, when sanguine children are put together in one group, they do not intensify each other's sanguinity but tone it down. And when in your

---

2. See *The Foundations of Human Experience* (previously *Study of Man*), Anthroposophic Press, Hudson, NY, 1996 and *Practical Advice to Teachers,* Rudolf Steiner Press, London, 1988 (at the end of the first lectures in each). In addition to these lectures and discussions with the teachers, Rudolf Steiner was giving other lectures simultaneously in order to prepare for the opening of the school the following month. See *The Spirit of the Waldorf School: Lectures Surrounding the Founding of the First Waldorf School, Stuttgart–1919*, Anthroposophic Press, Hudson, NY, 1995 (these lectures began August 24, 1919).

lessons you turn to the choleric children, the sanguine profit from what you say, and vice versa. As a teacher you must allow your own soul mood to influence the children, while the children of like temperaments are toning down each other's soul moods. Talking and chattering together signifies an inner desire to subdue each other, even the chattering that goes on during the breaks. The cholerics will chatter less when sitting together than they would when sitting with children of other temperaments. We must avoid viewing and assessing these things externally.

Right from the very beginning I would like to point out the importance of arranging your teaching in the most concentrated way possible. Only in this way can you consider all the things I have spoken of, especially the temperaments. Therefore we shall not have what is ordinarily called the "schedule." In this sense our method will be directly opposite to the ideal of modern materialistic education. In Bâle, for example, we hear of the forty-minute period. One forty-minute lesson is immediately followed by another, and this simply means that whatever occurred in the first forty minutes is immediately wiped out again, and fearful confusion is created in the minds of the children.

We must consider very carefully what subject is suitable for a particular age, and then we take this subject—perhaps reading—for awhile without interruption. That is, a child will learn reading every morning for six or eight weeks; after that writing will take its place and then arithmetic, so that for a certain period of time the child will concentrate on one subject. Thus, if I wanted to outline a scheme, our education would consist in this: whenever possible, as far as external arrangements will allow, we should begin the morning with reading and continue this for some weeks, then pass on to writing, and finally to arithmetic.

In such "main lessons" we should also include stories. In the first school year these will be mainly fairy tales. In the second year we try to introduce animal life in story form. From the fable we pass on to speaking of how the animals behave toward each other in real life. But in any case, our lessons will be arranged so that the attention of the children will be concentrated for several weeks on the same thing. Then at the end of the school year we allow time to recapitulate so that what was learned at the beginning will be revived. The only thing that will be kept apart and carried continuously is the artistic work. Either in the afternoons or, if there is enough time, in the mornings we should have art lessons, treating them as a special training of the will.

It would be ideal in school education if concentrated teaching, which require the child to exert the head forces, could be limited to an hour and a half a day. Then we could have another half hour for telling fairy tales—and besides that, it would always be possible to add about another hour and a half for artistic work. This would amount to no more than three and a half hours teaching in the day for children up to the age of twelve. Out of these three and a half hours we could then, on any given day, allow the short time necessary for the religion lesson, and in this way we could teach the children in relays. Thus, if we have a large number of children in one class we could arrange for one group of children from 7 A.M. to 10 A.M., and another group from 10:15 A.M. until 1:15 P.M., and in this way we could manage with the available classroom space.

Our ideal would be, therefore, not to occupy any child for longer than three and a half hours. Then the children would always be fresh, and our only other problem would be to think of what we could do with them in the school gardens when there are no lessons. They can play outside during the summer, but during the winter, when they have to be inside, it is difficult to keep them occupied all the time in the gymnasium. One eurythmy lesson and one gymnastics lesson should be arranged each week. But it is good to keep the children at school even when there are no lessons, so they can play and amuse themselves. I do not think it makes much difference if lessons are begun first thing in the morning or later, so that we could very well divide certain classes into two groups.

Now you must realize that there are all kinds of tasks before you. Over time we will have to discuss the whole organization of our work, but first let's take this question of story-telling lessons. It would be good if you could consider what you really want to foster in the children by means of these lessons. Our study of the general educational principles will give you what you need for the actual class teaching, but for the story-telling lessons you will have to find the material yourselves to be given to the children during all of their school life, from seven to fourteen years of age, in a free narrative style.[3]

To this end, in the initial school years you should have a number of fairy tales available. These must be followed by stories from the animal world in fables; then Bible stories taken as general history, apart from the actual religion lessons; then scenes from ancient, medieval, and modern history. You must also be prepared to tell about the different races and their various characteristics, which are connected with the natural phenomena of their own countries. After that you must move on to how the various races are mutually related to each other—Indians, Chinese, or Americans, and what their peculiarities are: in short, you must give the children information about the different peoples of the Earth. This is particularly necessary for our present age.

---

3. Seven to fourteen years of age was the original range in the Waldorf school.

These are the special tasks I wanted to give you today. You will then see how discussions can help us. All I wanted to do today was to lay down the general lines for our discussions.

During the session Rudolf Steiner had written up the following summary on the blackboard:

1. A fund of fairy tales
2. Stories from the animal realm in fables
3. Bible stories as part of general history (Old Testament)
4. Scenes from ancient history
5. Scenes from medieval history
6. Scenes from modern history
7. Stories of the various races and tribes
8. Knowledge of the races

---

*Questions and Answers*

*A question concerning the pictures used for sounds and letters—for example, the* f *in* fish, *mentioned in the first lecture of* Practical Advice to Teachers, *which was given in the morning.*

RUDOLF STEINER: One must find such things, these *pictures* for example, for oneself. Don't rely on what other people have already done. Put your own free, but controlled, imagination to work, and have faith in what you find for yourselves; you can do the same thing for letters that express motion, the letter *s* for example. Work it out for yourselves.

*A question about the treatment of melancholic children.*

RUDOLF STEINER: The teacher should view the melancholic child in this way: melancholic tendency arises when the soul-spirit of the human being cannot fully control the metabolic system. The nerve-sense human is the least spiritual part of a human being—it is the most physical. The least physical part is the metabolic human. The spiritual human is most firmly rooted in the metabolic organism, but nevertheless, it has realized itself least of all within it. The metabolic organism must be worked on more than any other. Thus, when the metabolic presents too many hindrances, the inner striving toward spirit is revealed in a brooding temperament.

When we deal with a melancholic children, we should try to arouse an interest in what they see around them; we should act, as much as possible, as though we were sanguine, and characterize the world accordingly. With sanguine children, on the other hand, we must be serious, with all inner earnestness, giving them clear strong pictures of the external world, which will leave an impression and remain in their minds.

Spirit has entered most into human beings in the nerve-sense system;[4] and spirit has entered least into the metabolic; spirit has the strongest tendency to penetrate into and to be absorbed by the nerve-sense system.

*A question about school books.*

RUDOLF STEINER: You will have to look at those commonly used. But the less we need to use books the better. We only need printed books when the children have to take public examinations. We have to be clear about how we want to reach our goal in education. Ideally we should have no examinations at all. The final exams are a compromise with the authorities. Prior to puberty, dread of examinations can become the driving impulse of the whole physiological and psychological constitution of the

---

4. That is, as *free* spirit, not absorbed in physical processes. On this important distinction see *The Foundations of Human Experience.*

child. The best thing would be to get rid of all examinations. The children would then become much more quick-witted.

The *temperament* gradually wears down its own corners; as the tenth year approaches the difference in temperaments will gradually be overcome. Boys and girls need not be separated; we only do this for the benefit of public opinion. Liaisons will be formed, which need not worry us, although we will be criticized for it. As long as the teacher has authority the teaching will not suffer.

Specialty teachers will be needed for the art subjects, which work on the will, and also for languages, which are taught apart from the Main Lesson. The subjects that the class teacher brings belong together as a whole, and the class teachers can base their work very largely on this unity. In all teaching they will work especially on the intellect and on the feelings.[5] The arts, gymnastics, eurythmy, drawing, and painting, all work on the will.

The teacher goes along in the school with the class. The teacher of the highest class (the eighth grade) then begins again with the lowest (the first grade).

---

5. The German word is *Gemüt,* which has no exact English equivalent. It expresses "the feeling mind" in the medieval sense—the mind coming from the heart, permeated with feeling, as expressed in an old poem:

> God be in my head,
> And in my understanding;
> God be in mine eyes,
> And in my looking;
> God be in my mouth,
> And in my speaking;
> God be in my *heart,*
> And in my *thinking*
> God be at mine end,
> And at my departing.

> *Anon. From a Sarum Primer of 1558.*

# Discussion Two

*A report was presented on the following questions: How is the sanguine temperament expressed in a child? How should it be treated?*

RUDOLF STEINER: This is where our work of individuating begins. We have said that we can group children according to temperament. In the larger groups children can all take part in the general drawing lesson, but by dividing them into smaller groups we can personalize to some extent. How is this individuating to be done? Copying will play a very small part, but in drawing you will try to awaken an inner feeling for form so that you can individuate. You will be able to differentiate by your choice of forms by taking either forms with straight lines or those with more movement in them—by taking simpler, clearer forms, or those with more detail. The more complicated, detailed forms would be used with the child whose temperament is sanguine. From the various temperaments you can learn how to teach each individual child.

*A report was given on the same theme.*

RUDOLF STEINER: We must also be very clear that there is no need to make our methods rigidly uniform, because, of course, one teacher can do something that is very good in a particular case, and another teacher something else equally good. So we need not strive for pedantic uniformity, but on the other hand we must adhere to certain important principles, which must be thoroughly comprehended.

The question about whether a sanguine child is difficult or easy to handle is very important. You must form your own opinion about this and you must be very clear. For example, suppose you have to teach or explain something to a sanguine child. The child has taken it in, but after some time you notice that the child has lost interest—attention has turned to something else. In this way the child's progress is hindered. What would you do if you noticed, when you were talking about a horse, for example, that after awhile the sanguine child was far away from the subject and was paying attention to something entirely different, so that everything you were saying passed unnoticed? What would you do with a child like this?

In such a case much depends on whether or not you can give individual treatment. In a large class many of your guiding principles will be difficult to carry out. But you will have the sanguine children together in a group, and then you must work on them by showing them the melancholic pattern. If there is something wrong in the sanguine group, turn to the melancholic group and then bring the melancholic temperament into play so that it acts as an antidote to the other. In teaching large numbers you must pay great attention to this. It's important that you should not only be serious and restful in yourself, but that you should also allow the serious restfulness of the melancholic children to act on the sanguine children, and vice versa.

Let's suppose you are talking about a horse, and you notice that a child in the sanguine group has not been paying attention for a long time. Now try to verify this by asking the child a question that will make the lack of attention apparent. Then try to verify that one of the children in the melancholic group is still thinking about some piece of furniture you were talking about quite awhile ago, even though you have been speaking about the horse during that time. Make this clear by saying to the sanguine child, "You see, you forgot the horse a long time ago, but your friend over there is still thinking about that piece of furniture!"

A real situation of this kind works very strongly. In this way children act correctively on each other. It is very effective when they come to see themselves through these means. The subconscious soul has a strong feeling that such lack of cooperation will prevent a continuation of social life. You must make good use of this unconscious element in the soul, because teaching large numbers of children can be an excellent way to progress if you let your pupils wear off each other's corners. To bring out the contrast you must have a very light touch and humor, so that the children see you are never annoyed nor bear a grudge against them—that things are revealed simply through your method of handling them.

*The phlegmatic child was spoken of.*

RUDOLF STEINER: What would you do if a phlegmatic child simply did not come out of herself or himself at all and nearly drove you to despair?

*Suggestions were presented for the treatment of temperaments from the musical perspective and by relating them to Bible history.*

Phlegmatics: Harmonium and piano; Harmony; Choral singing; The Gospel of Matthew; (variety)
Sanguines: Wind instruments; Melody; Whole orchestra; The Gospel of Luke; (Inwardness of soul)
Cholerics: Percussion and drum; Rhythm; Solo instruments; The Gospel of St. Mark; (Force, strength)
Melancholics: Stringed Instruments; Counterpoint; Solo singing; The Gospel of St. John; (Deepening of the spirit)

RUDOLF STEINER: Much of this is very correct, especially the choice of instruments and musical instruction. Equally good is the contrast of solo singing for the melancholic, the whole orchestra for the sanguine, and choral singing for the phlegmatic. All this is very good, and also the way you have related the temperaments to the four Evangelists. But it wouldn't be as good to delegate the four arts according to temperaments; it is precisely because art is multifaceted that any single art can bring harmony to each temperament.[1] Within each art the principle is correct, but I would not distribute the arts themselves in this way. For example, you could in some circumstances help a phlegmatic child very much through something that appeals to the child in dancing or painting. Thus the child would not be deprived of whatever might be useful in any of the various arts. In any single art it is possible to allocate the various branches and expressions of the art according to temperament. Whereas it is certainly necessary to prepare everything in the best way for individual children, it would not be good here to give too much consideration to the temperaments.

*An account was given about the phlegmatic temperament and it was stated that the phlegmatic child sits with an open mouth.*

RUDOLF STEINER: That is incorrect; the phlegmatic child will not sit with the mouth open but with a closed mouth and drooping lips. Through this kind of hint we can sometimes hit the nail on the head. It was very good that you touched on this, but as a rule it is not true that a phlegmatic child will sit with an open mouth, but just the opposite. This leads us back to the

---

1. The teacher who presented the above suggestions had also allocated particular arts to the various temperaments.

question of what to do with the phlegmatic child who is nearly driving us to despair. The ideal remedy would be to ask the mother to wake the child every day at least an hour earlier than the child prefers, and during this time (which you really take from the child's sleep) keep the child busy with all kinds of things. This will not hurt the child, who usually sleeps much longer than necessary anyway. Provide things to do from the time of waking up until the usual waking hour. That would be an ideal cure. In this way, you can overcome much of the child's phlegmatic qualities. It will not be possible very often to get parents to cooperate in this way, but much could be accomplished by carrying out such a plan.

You can however do the following, which is only a substitute but can help greatly. When your group of phlegmatics sit there (not with open mouths), and you go past their desks as you often do, you could do something like this: [Dr. Steiner jangled a bunch of keys]. This will jar them and wake them up. Their closed mouths would then open, and exactly at this moment when you have surprised them, you must try to occupy them for five minutes! You must rouse them, shake them out of their lethargy by some external means. By working on the unconscious you must combat this irregular connection between the etheric and physical bodies. You must continually find fresh ways to jolt the phlegmatics, thus changing their drooping lips to open mouths, and that means that you will be making them do just what they do not like doing. This is the answer when the phlegmatics drive you to despair, and if you keep trying patiently to shake up the phlegmatic group in this way, again and again, you will accomplish much.

*Question: Wouldn't it be possible to have the phlegmatic children come to school an hour earlier?*

RUDOLF STEINER: Yes, if you could do that, and also see that the children are wakened with some kind of noise, that would naturally be very good; it would be good to include the phlegmatic children among those who come earliest to school.[2] The important thing with the phlegmatic children is to engage their attention as soon as you have changed their soul mood.

*The subject of food in relation to the different temperaments was introduced.*

RUDOLF STEINER: On the whole, the main time for digestion should not be during school hours, but smaller meals would be insignificant; on the contrary, if the children have had their breakfast they can be more attentive than when they come to school on empty stomachs. If they eat too much—and this applies especially to phlegmatic children—you cannot teach them anything. Sanguine children should not be given too much meat, nor phlegmatic too many eggs. The melancholic children, on the other hand, can have a good mixed diet, but not too many roots or too much cabbage. For melancholic children diet is very individual, and you have to watch that. With sanguine and phlegmatic children it is possible to generalize.

*The melancholic temperament was spoken of.*

RUDOLF STEINER: That was very good. When you teach you will also have to realize that melancholic children get left behind easily; they do not keep up easily with others. I ask you to remember this also.

*The same theme was continued.*

---

2. This refers to the need for having school in shifts.

RUDOLF STEINER: It was excellent that you stressed the importance of the teacher's attitude toward the melancholic children. Moreover, they are slow in the birth of the etheric body, which otherwise becomes free during the change of teeth. Therefore, these children have a greater aptitude for imitation; if they have become fond of you, everything you do in front of them will make a lasting impression on them. You must use the fact that they retain the principle of imitation longer than others.

*A further report on the melancholic temperament.*

RUDOLF STEINER: You will find it very difficult to treat the melancholic temperament if you fail to consider one thing that is almost always present: the melancholic lives in a strange condition of self-deception. Melancholics have the opinion that their experiences are peculiar to themselves. The moment you can bring home to them that others also have these or similar experiences, they will to some degree be cured, because they then perceive they are not the singularly interesting people they thought themselves to be. They are prepossessed by the illusion that they are very exceptional as they are.

When you can impress a melancholic child by saying, "Come on now, you're not so extraordinary after all; there are plenty of people like you, who have had similar experiences," then this will act as a very strong corrective to the impulses that lead to melancholy. Because of this it is good to make a point of presenting them with the biographies of great persons; they will be more interested in these individuals than in external nature. Such biographies should be used especially to help these children over their melancholy.

*Two teachers spoke about the choleric temperament. Rudolf Steiner then drew the following figures on the board:*

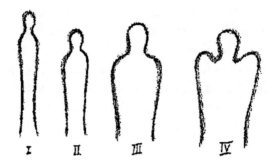

What do we see in these figures? They depict another characterization of the four temperaments. The melancholic children are as a rule tall and slender; the sanguine are the most normal; those with more protruding shoulders are the phlegmatic children; and those with a short stout build so that the head almost sinks down into the body are choleric.

Both Michelangelo and Beethoven have a combination of melancholic and choleric temperaments. Please remember particularly that when we are dealing with the temperament of a child, as teachers we should not assume that a certain temperament is a fault to be overcome. We must recognize the temperament and ask ourselves the following question: How should we treat it so that the child may reach the desired goal in life—so that the very best may be drawn out of the temperament and with the help of their own temperaments, children can reach their goals.

Particularly in the case of the choleric temperament, we would help very little by trying to drive it out and replacing it with something else. Indeed, much arises from the life and passion of choleric people—especially when we look at history and find that many things would have happened differently had there been no cholerics. So we must make it our task to bring the child, regardless of the temperament, to the goal in life belonging to that child's nature.

For the choleric you should use as much as possible fictional situations, describing situations you have made up for the occasion, and that you bring to the child's attention. If, for example, you have a child with a temper, describe such situations to the child and deal with them yourself, treating them in a choleric way. For example, I would tell a choleric child about a wild fellow whom I had met, whom I would then graphically describe to the child. I would get roused and excited about him, describing how I treated him, and what I thought of him, so that the child sees temper in someone else, in a fictitious way the child sees it in action. In this way you will bring together the inner forces of such a child, whose general power of understanding is thus increased.

*The teachers asked Rudolf Steiner to relate the scene between Napoleon and his secretary.*

Rudolf Steiner: For this you would first have to get permission from the Ministry of Housing! Through describing such a scene the choleric element would have to be brought out. But a scene such as I just mentioned must be described by the teacher so that the *choleric* element is apparent. This will always arouse the forces of a choleric child, with whom you can then continue to work. It would be ideal to describe such a situation to the choleric group in order to arouse their forces, the effect of which would then last a few days. During that few days the children will have no difficulty taking in what you want to teach them. Otherwise they fume inwardly against things that they should be getting through their understanding.

Now I would like you to try something: we should have a record of what we have been saying about the treatment of temperaments, and so I should like to ask Miss B. to write a comprehensive survey (approximately six pages) of the characteristics of the different temperaments and how to treat them, based on everything I have spoken about here. Also, I will ask Mrs. E. to imagine she has two groups of children in front of her, sanguine and melancholic and then, in a kind of drawing lesson, to use simple designs, varied according to sanguine and melancholic children. I will ask Mr. T. to do the same thing with drawings for phlegmatic and choleric children; and please bring these tomorrow when you have prepared them.

Then I will ask, let us say, Miss A., Miss D., and Mr. R. to deal with a problem: Imagine that you have to tell the same fairy tale twice—not twice in the same way, but clothed in different sentences, and so on. The first time pay more attention to the sanguine and the second time to the melancholic children, so that both get something from it.

Then I ask that perhaps Mr. M. and Mr. L. work at the difficult task of giving two separate descriptions of an animal or animal species, first for the cholerics and then for the phlegmatics. And I will ask Mr. O., Mr. N., and perhaps with the help of Mr. U. to solve the problem of how to consider the four temperaments in arithmetic.

When you consider something like the temperaments in working out your lessons, you must remember above all that the human being is constantly *becoming*, always changing and developing. This is something that we as teachers must have always in our consciousness—that the human being is constantly *becoming*, that in the course of life human beings are subject to metamorphosis. And just as we should give serious consideration to the temperamental dispositions of individual children, so we must also reflect on the element of growth, this becoming, so that we come to see that all children are primarily sanguine, even if they are also phlegmatic or choleric in certain things. All adolescents, boys and girls, are really cholerics, and if this is not so at this time of life it shows an unhealthy development. In mature life a person is melancholic and in old age phlegmatic.

This again sheds some light on the question of temperaments, because here you have something particularly necessary to remember at the present time. In our day we love to make fixed, sharply defined concepts. In reality, however, everything is interwoven so that, even while you are saying that a person is made up of head, breast, and limb organizations, you must be clear that these three really interpenetrate one another. Thus a choleric child is only *mostly* choleric, a sanguine *mostly* sanguine, and so on. Only at the age of adolescence can one become completely choleric. Some people remain adolescents till they die, because they preserve this age of adolescence within themselves throughout life. Nero and Napoleon never outgrew the age of youth. This shows us how qualities that follow each other during growth can still—through further change—permeate each other again.

What is the poet's productivity actually based on—or indeed any spiritually creative power? How does it happen that a man, for example, can become a poet? It is because he has preserved throughout his whole life certain qualities that belonged to early manhood and childhood. The more such a man remains "young," the more aptitude he has for the art of poetry. In a certain sense it is a misfortune for such a man if he cannot keep some of the qualities of youth, something of a sanguine nature, his whole life through. It is very important that teachers can become sanguine out of their own resolve. And it is moreover tremendously important for teachers to remember this so they may cherish this happy disposition of the child as something of particular value.

All creative qualities in life—everything that fosters the spiritual and cultural side of the social organism—all of this depends on the *youthful* qualities in a human being. These things will be accomplished by those who have preserved the temperament of youth. All economic life, on the other hand, depends on the qualities of old age finding their way into people, even when they are young. This is because all economic judgment depends on experience. Experience is best gained when certain qualities of old age enter into people, and the old person is indeed a phlegmatic. Those business people prosper most whose other attributes and qualities have an added touch of the phlegmatic, which really already bears the stamp of old age. That is the secret of very many business people—that in addition to their other good qualities as business people, they also have something of old age about them, especially in the way they manage their businesses. In the business world, a person who only developed the sanguine temperament would only get as far as the projects of youth, which are never finished. A choleric who remains at the stage of youth might spoil what was done earlier in life through policies adopted later. The melancholic cannot be a business person anyway, because a harmonious development in business life is connected with a quality of old age. A harmonious temperament, along with some of the phlegmatic's unexcitability is the best combination for business life.

You see, if you are thinking of the future of humankind you must really notice such things and consider them. A person of thirty who is a poet or painter is also something more than "a person of thirty," because that individual at the same time has the qualities of childhood and youth within, which have found their way into the person's being. When people are creative you can see how another being lives in them, in which they have remained more or less childlike, in which the essence of childhood still dwells. Everything I have exemplified must become the subject of a new kind of psychology.

# Discussion Three

*Someone told the story of "Mary's Child," first for melancholic and then for sanguine children.*

RUDOLF STEINER: I think in the future you will have to pay more attention to your articulation. The two versions, as you gave them, were too much alike. The difference must also lie in the articulation. If you bring out these details more emphatically you will not fail to impress the melancholic children. For the sanguines I would introduce more pauses into the story, especially at the beginning, so that the children are compelled to listen to you again each time their attention wanders. But now I would like to ask how you would apply these stories when you are actually teaching? Imagine yourselves standing in front of the class; what would you do? I would advise you to tell the story in the melancholic version and then have it retold by a sanguine child and vice versa.

*A person comments: First, I think it would be advisable to seat the sanguine children directly in front of the teacher so they may be constantly within view, whereas melancholic children should be sitting where they like as much as possible.*

RUDOLF STEINER: An excellent suggestion.

*The individual who commented then related the story of "The Long-tailed Monkey," first in a style for the sanguine and then for the melancholic children, adding the remark that melancholic children do not want to hear too many sad stories.*

RUDOLF STEINER: You should also remember that, but the contrasting styles were good. Now I think we can go on to how we should make further use of these things later. I would not decide which child is to tell the story, but after a day or two I would say (in a lively way): "Now listen! You can choose for yourselves which part of the story you would like to retell. Then the next day or the day after that any child who wants to can come out and tell a portion of the story to the class.

*Someone else told another story in two versions.*

RUDOLF STEINER: You all have the feeling, don't you, that something like this can be done in various ways. Now it is really very important, particularly for those who want to work as teachers, to get rid of the habit of unnecessary criticism. As a teacher you should develop a strong feeling for this; you should definitely be conscious that it is not a question of always trying to improve on what has already been done. A thing can be good in a variety of ways. And so I think it will be good to view what has been presented as something that can certainly be done as you have proposed.

But there is one thing I would like to add. In all three stories I think I noticed that the first rendering, both in style and purpose, was the better of the two. Which did you work out first in your mind, Miss A? Which did you feel you could do better? [It was determined that the version worked out first was for the melancholic temperament, and this was the better of the two]. I would now like to recommend that all three of you work out a version for the phlegmatic child. This version is very important from the perspective of style. But if possible please try to work this out tentatively today, then sleep on it and come to your final decision about the style tomorrow. It has been found by experience that when you have something like this to do, you can only discover its new form in a different spirit when, after the preparation, you allow it to pass through a period of sleep. On Monday bring us a version for the phlegmatics, but prepare it first and then later work out its final form. Having the Sunday in between will make this possible.

*Someone showed a drawing, a design in blue and yellow for a melancholic child. Dr. Steiner drew the same design in green and red for a sanguine child.*

RUDOLF STEINER: Now you can say to the children: This blue and yellow one can be seen best when it is getting dark; you take it into sleep with you, because that is the color with which you can appear before God. This one, the green and red one, can meet your eyes when you awake. You can gaze at it when you wake up in the morning and enjoy it for the rest of the day!

*A drawing for a sanguine child was then displayed, red on a white ground. Dr. Steiner drew the same design for a melancholic child, long and thin on a black ground. Dr. Steiner called the impudent form sticking out a "little kicker."*[1]

RUDOLF STEINER: In the design for the melancholics this little creature withdraws into the form. Here you see the contrast, a kind of contrast where you would primarily use the colors in order to work on one child or another, and you should certainly show the same thing twice. What would you say to the children?

---

1. *Kickerling* = indicating a small football player.

*I would ask them which one they liked best.*

RUDOLF STEINER: You would then make your own discoveries! You would recognize the sanguine children from their joy in this contrast of colors. You should not miss the opportunity to use simple forms like these for the children.

*Someone recommended forms pointed outward for the choleric:*

to be changed to an enclosed form

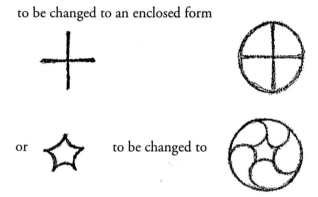

or                         to be changed to

*For the phlegmatic he recommended the opposite way, to start from the circle and have figures drawn inside it or to break up a circle in some way:*

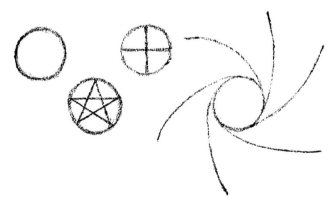

RUDOLF STEINER: For the phlegmatic child I would add the following in this method. I should say:

"Look, here is a circle. You like that don't you?

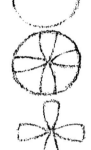

"But now I'll draw something else for you:

"And if I simply take away the circle, then you have the form as it should be. You must get into the habit of not muddling things up together."

By drawing things and rubbing them out again the phlegmatic child can be torn out of his phlegma. Now I will also ask you, Frau E., to work out the same design for other temperaments again, making use of the method of sleeping over what you have done.

*A description of a gorilla was given in two versions.*

RUDOLF STEINER: Of course nothing can be said against your inventing things without depending on any particular naturalists, although you may very well get suggestions from them. I would ask you, however, to awaken a closer contact with your students when you tell them a story of this kind. It would also be possible to use a long story and to make an impression with that. You must, however, not be absorbed in your own thoughts, but maintain closer contact with your students. If you are too absorbed in yourself you could easily lose contact with the children.

*A horse was described for phlegmatic and choleric children.*

RUDOLF STEINER: In giving descriptions of animals it is especially important that, in every detail, we should remain clear in our minds that a human being is really the whole animal kingdom. The animal kingdom in its entirety is humankind. You cannot, of course, present ideas of this kind to the children theoretically, and you certainly should not do so.

Let's suppose, however, that someone has to work out in detail the subject Mr. L. introduced, and also distinguish between the phlegmatic and choleric groups. The phlegmatics are not as easily interested and they are not likely to remember much of what you tell them about an ordinary animal, such as a horse. They have seen horses often enough that they have very little interest in them.[2] But it is important to focus their attention, so I should say to the phlegmatic children, "Well now, what is the real difference between you and a horse? Let's take some minor differences. You all have a foot like this, don't you? Here are the toes, here is the heel and here is the instep.

"Now look at a horse's foot. This is the hind foot of a horse. Where are the toes? Where is the heel? And where is the ankle? With you the knee is farther up. Where is the knee of a horse?

---

2. This statement may not apply to the children of today, as it did in 1919.

Now look, here are the toes, the heel is right up there and the knee farther up still. It is very different. Just imagine how different a horse's foot looks from yours." You will now find that this will surprise the phlegmatic child into alertness, and what you have said will not be forgotten.

For the choleric children I would tell a story about how a child meets a horse out in the woods somewhere. The horse is running; and far behind, running after it, there is a man from whom it has bolted, and the child has to catch the horse by the bridle. If I know I have a choleric child before me I can try to show how the child should do this, how to get hold of the bridle. To get the child's fantasy working to discover how the horse should be caught is a very good thing. Even a choleric child feels a little nervous about such a procedure, but you are meeting the need of the choleric temperament when you expect the child to do it. Such a child will become a little disconcerted and less arrogant. Something is expected of the child that can only be expected of a choleric child.

I would also like to say that, especially at first, you should make all such stories very short. So I will ask Mr. M. in this case to tell his story for sanguine and melancholic children, but let both stories be exceedingly short. Mr. L., you could do the same but choose particular incidents that will be remembered and serve to arouse the children's eager interest.

We must realize that we should use the subject matter of our teaching primarily to capture the child's powers of will, feeling, and thought; it is not so important to us that the children remember what they are told, but that they develop their soul faculties.

*Someone spoke of how to consider the four temperaments in arithmetic, but explained that he had not really managed to work this out properly.*

RUDOLF STEINER: I had foreseen that, because this problem is very difficult. You will have to sleep on it very thoroughly.

But please take the following as a fresh problem. Imagine to yourself a class in which there are children of eight and nine years old. In the teaching of the future it will, of course, be important that we develop as many social instincts as possible, that we educate the social will. Now imagine three children of whom one is a pronounced phlegmatic, another a pronounced choleric, and the third a pronounced melancholic. I will say nothing about their other qualities. Let's suppose that in the third or fourth week after school had begun these children come to you and say, "None of the other children can stand me!" Immediately it would be obvious that these are the "Cinderellas" of the class, and all the other children are inclined to avoid them. By Monday I would like you to think over how the teacher can best try to remedy this evil. Please give your whole mind to thinking this through, and view it as a very important educational problem.

# Discussion Four

RUDOLF STEINER: We will now continue the work we have set out to do, and we will pass on to what will be said about how to deal with arithmetic from the perspective of the temperaments. We must primarily consider what procedure we should follow in teaching arithmetic.

*Someone showed how to explain a fraction by breaking a piece of chalk.*

RUDOLF STEINER: First, I have just one thing to say: I would not use chalk, because it is a great pity to break chalk. I would choose something less valuable. A bit of wood or something like that would do, wouldn't it? It is not good to accustom young children to destroy useful things.

*Question: Does a child who slouches and lacks a proper vertical position find it more difficult to understand spatial and geometrical forms because of such a problem?*

RUDOLF STEINER: Not to any perceptible degree. Things of this kind depend more on the tendencies found in the construction of the human organism rather than on the build of an individual. This was once brought very forcibly to my attention after a lecture in Munich. I had explained in the lecture that it has a certain significance for the whole structure of the human being that the backbone is in line with the diameter of the Earth, while the

line of the animal's back is at a right angle to it. Afterward a
learned doctor from Karlsruhe came and asserted that when a
person is asleep the spine is in a horizontal position! I replied,
"It's not a question of whether a person can move the backbone
into various positions, but that the whole human structure is
arranged architecturally so that the backbone is ordinarily vertical, although it can be placed at a slant or any other position."

If you did not consider this you could never understand how
certain potentials found in the intellect appear, even when the
senses themselves are not active—for example, in someone born
blind. The human being is constructed so that the intellect has
certain tendencies in the direction of the eyes, and thus, even in
the case of those born blind, it is still possible to evoke mental
images that are connected with the eyes, such as in the case of
someone like the blind Helen Keller. What is important is the
*tendency*, the general dispositions of the human organism, rather
than what may be the result of a chance situation here or there.

I would now like to add the following to what was said. It is
not so much a question of criticizing these things, because that
can always be done. What matters is that things of this kind are
brought up and that we try to understand them.

Let's start with addition, and first see what our view of
addition should be. Let's suppose I have some beans or a heap
of elderberries. For our present task I will assume that the
children can count, which indeed they must learn to do first.
A child counts them and finds there are 27. "Yes," I say. "27—
that is the sum." We proceed from the sum, not from the
addenda. You can follow the psychological significance of this
in my theory of knowledge.[1] We must now divide the whole

---

1. See Rudolf Steiner, *Goethe's World View*, and *The Science of Knowing:
Outline of an Epistemology Implicit in the Goethean World View*, both
Mercury Press, Spring Valley, NY, 1992 and 1988.

into the addenda, into parts or into little heaps. We will have one heap of, let's say, 12 elderberries, another heap of 7, still another of say 3, and one more, let's say 5; this will represent the whole number of our elderberries: 27 = 12 + 7 + 3 + 5.

We work out our arithmetical process from the sum total 27. I would allow this process to be done by several children with a pronounced phlegmatic temperament. You will gradually come to realize that this kind of addition is particularly suited to the phlegmatics. Then, since the process can be reversed, I would call on some choleric children, and gather the elderberries together again, this time arranging them so that 5 + 3 + 7 + 12 = 27. In this way the choleric children do the reverse process. But addition in itself is the arithmetical rule particularly suited to phlegmatic children.

Now I choose one of the melancholic children and say, "Here is a little pile of elderberries. Count them for me." The child discovers that there are, let's say, 8. Now, I say, "I don't want 8, I only want 3. How many elderberries must you take away to leave me only 3?" The child will discover that 5 must be removed. Subtraction in this form is the one of the four rules especially suited to melancholic children.

Then I call on a sanguine child to do the reverse process. I ask what has been taken away, and I have this child tell me that if I take 5 from 8, I'll have 3 left. Thus, the sanguine child does the reverse arithmetical process. I would only like to add that the melancholic children generally have a special connection with subtraction when done as I have described.

Now I take a child from the sanguine group. Again I put down a pile of elderberries, but I must be sure the numbers fit. I must arrange it beforehand, otherwise we find ourselves involved in fractions. I have the child count out 56 elderberries. "Now look; here I have 8 elderberries, so now tell me how many times you find 8 elderberries contained in 56." So you see that multiplication leads to a dividing up. The child finds that the answer is 7. Now I let the sum be done in *reverse* by a melancholic child and say, "This time I do not want to know how often 8 is contained in 56, but what number is contained 7 times in 56." I always allow the reverse process to be done by the opposite temperament.

Next I introduce the choleric to division, from the smaller number to the greater, by saying, "Look, here you have a little pile of 8; I want you to tell me what number contains 8 seven times." Now the child must find the answer: 56, in a pile of 56. Then I have the phlegmatic children work out the opposite process: ordinary division. The former is the way I use division for the choleric child, because the rule of arithmetic for the choleric children is mainly in this form division.

By continuing in this way I find it possible to use the four rules of arithmetic to arouse interest among the four temperaments. Adding is related to the phlegmatic temperament, subtracting to the melancholic, multiplying to the sanguine, and dividing—working back to the dividend—to the choleric. I ask you to consider this, following what N. has been telling us.

It is very important not to continue working in a singular way, doing nothing but addition for six months, then subtraction, and so on; but whenever possible, take all four arithmetical rules fairly quickly, one after another, and then *practice them all*—but at first only up to around the number 40. So we shall not teach arithmetic as it is done in an ordinary curriculum. By practicing these four rules, however, they can be assimilated almost simultaneously. You will find that this saves a great deal of time, and in this way the children can work one rule in with another. Division is connected with subtraction, and multiplication is really only a repetition of addition, so you can even change things around and give subtraction, for example, to the choleric child.

*It was suggested that one begin with solid geometry.*

RUDOLF STEINER: With adults it is possible to begin with solids, but why should you want to go from solids to plane surfaces with a child? You see, three-dimensional space is never easy to picture, least of all for a child. You cannot impart anything to a child but a vague idea of space. Indeed, the child's imagination will suffer if expected to imagine solid bodies.

You are assuming that the solid is the actual thing and the line abstract; but this is not so. A triangle is in itself something very concrete; it exists in space. Children see things mainly in surfaces. It is an act of violence to force a child into the third dimension, the idea of depth. If children are to apply their imagination to a solid, then they must first have the necessary elements within to build up this imaginative picture. For example, children must really have a clear picture of a line and a triangle before a tetrahedron can be understood. It is better for them to first have a real mental picture of a triangle; the triangle is an *actuality*, not merely an abstraction taken from the solid.

I would recommend that you teach geometry, not as solid geometry first, but as plane geometry, giving figures with plane surfaces between them; this is preferable, because children like to use their powers of understanding for such things; beginning with plane geometry will support them. You can add further to the effect by connecting it with drawing lessons. Children can draw a triangle relatively early, and you should not wait too long before having them copy what they see.
The figure shown yesterday was repeated, this time for a choleric child and for a phlegmatic child.

RUDOLF STEINER: That is a very good design for the choleric child. For the phlegmatic child I would prefer to make it speckled, I would rather have it checkered. It would be possible to use your design, but it would not arouse the phlegmatic child's attention enough.

*The drawings for the melancholic and the sanguine child were presented.*

RUDOLF STEINER: In using this method you will find that the needs of the sanguine and melancholic child can be met in the following ways. For the sanguine you should constantly make use of varied repetition. You might have the child draw a design like this:

And then three more like it:

and then one more, so that the emphasis is on repetition:

For the melancholic child it would be good to give a design in which careful thought plays some part.

Fig. a     Fig. b

Suppose you have a melancholic child first draw a form like this (figure a), and then the counter-form (figure b), so that they complement one another. This will arouse the child's imagination. I will shade the original form like this (a) and the opposite form like this (b) and you will see that what is shaded in one form would be left blank in the other. If you think of the blank part as filled in, you would get the first form again. In this way the outer forms in the second drawing are the opposite of the inner, and this design is the opposite of those based on repetition. Choose something requiring thought and connected with observation for the melancholic children, and something in which repetition plays a part (creepers, tendrils, and so on) for the sanguine children.

*The story of "Mary's Child" was told in the style for phlegmatic children.*

RUDOLF STEINER: It is important to cultivate well-articulated speech and then help the children to get out of their dialect.[2] Frau Dr. Steiner will demonstrate.

*Someone told the story of "The Long-Tailed Monkey" for phlegmatic children.*

RUDOLF STEINER: For a story of this kind there are certain aids to storytelling that I would suggest you use. Just for the phlegmatics it would be good to pause occasionally mid-sentence, look at the children, and use the pause to let the imagination work. You can arouse their curiosity at critical points so that they can think on in advance a little and complete the picture for themselves. "The king's daughter ... was ... very beautiful ... but ... she was not equally ... good." This use of pauses in narration works strongest with phlegmatic children.

*A fairy story was told for phlegmatic children.*

---

2. This does not imply that Rudolf Steiner was unaware of the importance of dialect in its right place.

RUDOLF STEINER: You must make use of a moment of surprise and curiosity.

*Someone told an animal story for sanguine children about a horse, a donkey, and a camel. "Which do you like best, the horse or the donkey?"*

RUDOLF STEINER: Some melancholics will prefer the donkey. With these descriptions of animals I would ask you to remember that, as far as possible, they should lead the child to observe animals, for descriptions of this kind can contain true natural history.

*Someone else told the story of a monkey who escaped into the rafters—first for sanguines and then for melancholics.*

RUDOLF STEINER: Yes, in certain cases that would make a very good impression on the melancholic children, but here also it is my opinion that you could develop it a little further in order to encourage animal observation as such.

I would like to remind you that consideration of the child's temperament should not be neglected, but you can safely use the first three to five weeks to observe the temperaments of your pupils and then divide them into groups as spoken of here.

It would also be good to consider the extremes of the various temperaments. Goethe's world view led him to express the beautiful idea that one can understand the normal by studying the abnormal. Goethe views an abnormal plant—a misshapen plant—and from the nature of the malformation he learns to understand the normal plant. In the same way you can find the connections between the absolutely normal and the malformations of the body-soul nature, and you yourselves can find the way from the temperaments to what is abnormal in the soul life.

If the *melancholic* temperament becomes abnormal and does not remain within the boundaries of the soul, but rather encroaches on the body, then *insanity* arises. Insanity is the abnormal development of a predominantly melancholic temperament. The abnormal development of the phlegmatic temperament is *mental deficiency*. The abnormal development of the sanguine is *foolishness*, or *stupidity*. The abnormal development of the choleric is *rage*. When a person is in an emotional state you will sometimes see these attacks of insanity, mental deficiency, foolishness, or rage arising from otherwise normal soul conditions. It is indeed necessary that you focus your attention and observation on the entire soul life.

Now we will move on to the solution of our other problem. I said: Suppose that you, my friends, had children of eight or nine years old in your class. What would you do if, three or four weeks after the beginning of term, you noticed that a phlegmatic, a choleric, and a melancholic child were, to some extent, becoming the three "Cinderellas" of the class, so that all the others pushed them around and no one wanted to play with them and so on? If this had happened, what would you as teachers do about it?

*Various teachers expressed opinions.*

RUDOLF STEINER: You should never allow the children to inform against each other; you must find other ways of discovering what has caused them to be "Cinderellas." As teachers, you see, you will often find that you have to help raise the children. If they get into all sorts of naughty ways, their fathers and mothers will come and say, for example, "My child tells lies." You would seldom go wrong to give this advice: say to the parents, "Imagine a case, a story, in which an untruthful child is placed in a ridiculous position—where the child, because of lying, is led into a situation that appears absurd even to the child. If you tell the child a story of this kind, and then another, and still another like it, you will as a rule cure your child of the tendency to lie."

Similarly, you will find it helpful to insert into a story everything that has been said about the three "Cinderellas," everything you can hear and discover about these children, and then you can tell this story to the whole class. The effect of this will be that the three "Cinderellas" will be somewhat comforted and the others somewhat ashamed. If you do this you will certainly find that, even at the first attempt, and even more after the second, you will succeed in restoring a friendly, social atmosphere, a mutual sympathy among the children. You should continue with a similar story throughout the term.

Tomorrow we will take another case that also happens sometimes, which certainly *cannot* be treated by telling a story that comforts some of the children and shames the others. Suppose you had children of eight or nine years old in your class, and one of these small fries had discovered a particularly mischievous trick. These things do happen. It had been learned outside the school and succeeded in infecting all the others so that the whole class was at it during recess.

An ordinary schoolmaster would go to the extreme of punishing the whole class, but I hope that by tomorrow you will think of a more rational—that is a more effective—method, because this old way of punishing places the teacher in the wrong relationship with the children, and this will not fail to have an effect. The aftereffect is not good.

I have a special case in mind that really happened, where a certain teacher did not act very wisely. One little rascal had conceived the idea of spitting on the ceiling and had actually succeeded. It was a long time before the teacher discovered the culprit. He could not pick out any one child, because they had all done it; the whole classroom was damaged.

Please think over this case of moral delinquency by tomorrow. All you really know is that the whole class had been infected. You cannot begin with the assumption that you know who the ringleader was. You will have to consider whether it wouldn't be better to give up all thought of discovering the culprit by getting the children to tell on each other. How would you act in this case?

# Discussion Five

RUDOLF STEINER: It is most important that, along with all our other work, we should cultivate clear articulation. This has a kind of influence, a certain effect. I have here some sentences that I formulated for another occasion; they have no especially profound meaning, but are constructed so that the speech organs are activated in every kind of movement, organically. I would like you to pass these sentences around and repeat them in turn without embarrassment so that by constant practice they may make our speech organs flexible; we can have these organs do gymnastics, so to speak. Mrs. Steiner will say the sentences first as it should be done artistically, and I will ask each one of you to repeat them after her. These sentences are not composed according to sense and meaning, but in order to "do gymnastics" with the speech organs.[1]

> Dart may these boats through darkening gloaming
> Name neat Norman on nimble moody mules

The *N* is constantly repeated, but in different combinations of letters, and so the speech organ can do the right gymnastic

---

1. Elsewhere, Steiner stated: "In giving artistic shape and form to speech, healthy cooperation and harmonization of body, soul, and spirit manifests. The body shows whether it can incorporate the spirit correctly; the soul reveals whether the spirit truly lives in it; and the spirit is vividly present, working directly into the physical." *Creative Speech*, Rudolf Steiner Press, London, 1978, p. 33. The original German speech exercises may be found in the appendix.

exercises. At one point two *N*s come together; you must stop longer over the first *N* in "*on nimble.*"

Rattle me more and more rattles now rightly

In this way you can activate the speech organs with the right gymnastics.

I would recommend that you take particular care to find your way into the very forms of the sounds and the forms of the syllables; see that you really grow into these forms, so that you consciously speak each sound, that you lift *each* sound into consciousness. It is a common weakness in speech that people just glide over the sounds, whereas speech is there to be understood. It would even be better to first bring an element of caricature into your speech by emphasizing syllables that should not be emphasized at all. Actors, for example, practice saying *friendly* instead of *friendly*! You must pronounce each letter consciously. It would even be good for you to do something like Demosthenes did, though perhaps not regularly. You know that, when he could not make any progress with his speaking, he put pebbles on his tongue and through practice strengthened his voice to the degree that it could be heard over a rushing river; this he did to acquire a delivery that the Athenians could hear.

. . . . . . . .

I will now ask Miss B. to introduce the question of temperaments. Since the individual child must be our primary consideration in teaching, it is proper that we study the basis of the temperaments with the maximum care. Naturally when we have a class it is not possible to treat each child individually. But you can give much individual treatment by having on one side, let's say, the phlegmatics and melancholics, and the sanguine and choleric children on the other side; you can have them take part in a lively interchange, turning now to the group of one temperament, and then calling on another group for answers, saying this to one group and that to another. In this way individualization happens on its own in the class.

*A comprehensive picture was presented of the temperaments and their treatment.*

RUDOLF STEINER: You have given a good account of what was spoken of in our conversations together on this subject. But you may be going too far when you assert, with regard to the melancholic temperament, that it has a decided inclination toward piety. There is only one little word lacking: "often." It is also just possible that the melancholic disposition in children is rooted in pronounced egoism, and in no way has a religious tendency. With adults you can leave out the little word "often," but in young children the melancholic element often masks a pronounced egoism. Melancholic children are often dependent on atmospheric conditions; the weather often effects the melancholic temperament. The sanguine children are also dependent on atmospheric conditions, but more in their moods, in the soul, whereas the melancholic children are affected more unconsciously by the weather in the physical body.

If I were to go into this question in detail from the standpoint of spiritual science, I would have to show you how the childish temperament is actually connected with karma, how in the child's temperament something really appears that could be described as the consequence of experiences in previous lives on Earth. Let's take the concrete example of a man who is obliged in one life to be very interested in himself. He is lonely and is thus forced to be interested in himself. Because he is frequently absorbed in himself, the force of circumstances causes him to be inclined to unite his soul very closely with the structure of his physical body, and in the next incarnation he brings with him a bodily nature keenly alive to the conditions of the outer world. He becomes a sanguine individual. Thus, it can happen that when someone has been compelled to live alone in one incarnation, which would have retarded the person's progress, this is adjusted in the next life through becoming a sanguine, with the ability to notice everything in the surroundings. We must not view karma from a moral but from a causal perspective. When a child is properly educated, it may be of great benefit to the child's life to be a sanguine, capable of observing the outer world. Temperament is connected, to a remarkable degree, with the whole life and soul of a person's previous incarnation.

*Dr. Steiner was asked to explain the changes of temperaments that can occur during life, from youth to maturity.*

RUDOLF STEINER: If you remember a course of lectures that I once gave in Cassel about the Gospel of St. John, you will recall the remarks I made concerning the relationship of a child to his or her parents.[2] It was stated there that the *father-principle* works very strongly in the physical body and the I, and that the *mother-principle* predominates in the etheric and astral bodies. Goethe divined this truth when he wrote the beautiful words:

From my father I have my stature [connected with the physical body] and the serious conduct of life [connected with the I], from my dear mother my happy nature [connected with the etheric body] and joy in creative fantasy [connected with the astral body].

---

2. *The Gospel of St. John: And Its Relation to the Other Gospels*, Anthroposophic Press, Hudson, NY, 1982.

There is extraordinary wisdom in these words. What lives in the human being is mixed and mingled in a remarkable way. Humankind is an extremely complicated being. A definite relationship exists in human beings between the I and the physical body, and again a relationship between the etheric body and the astral body. Thus, the predominance of one can pass over into the predominance of another during the course of life. For example, in the melancholic temperament the predominance of the I passes into the predominance of the physical body, and in a choleric person it even cuts across inheritance and passes from the mother element to the father element, because the preponderance of the astral passes over into a preponderance of the I.

In the melancholic temperament the I predominates in the child, the physical body in the adult. In the sanguine temperament the etheric body predominates in the child and the astral body in the adult. In the phlegmatic temperament the physical body predominates in the child and the etheric body in the adult. In the choleric temperament the astral body predominates in the child, the I in the adult. But you can only arrive at a true view of such things when you strictly remember that you cannot arrange them in a tabulated form, and the higher you come into spiritual regions, the less this will be possible.

*The observation was expressed that a similar change can be found in the sequence of names of the characters in* The Guardian of the Threshold *and* The Souls' Awakening.[3]

3. See Rudolf Steiner, *The Four Mystery Plays: The Portal of Initiation, The Soul's Probation, The Guardian of the Threshold,* and *The Souls' Awakening,* trans. Adam Bittleston, Rudolf Steiner Press, London, 1983. The four plays will be published individually; see *The Souls' Awakening: Soul and Spiritual Events in Dramatic Scenes,* trans. Ruth and Hans Pusch, Anthroposophic Press, Hudson, NY, 1995 (the other plays will follow).

RUDOLF STEINER: There is a change there that is definitely in accordance with the facts; these Mystery Plays must be taken theoretically as little as possible. I cannot say anything if the question is put theoretically, because I have always had these characters before me just as they are, purely objectively. They have all been taken from real life. Recently, on another occasion, I said here that Felix Balde[4] was a real person living in Trumau, and the old shoemaker who had known the archetype of Felix is called Scharinger, from Münchendorf. Felix still lives in the tradition of the village there. In the same way all these characters whom you find in my Mystery Plays are actual individual personalities.

*Question: In speaking of a folk temperament can you also speak of someone as belonging to the temperament of one's nation? And a further question: Is the folk temperament expressed in the language?*

RUDOLF STEINER: What you said first is right, but your second suggestion is not quite correct. It is possible to speak of a folk temperament in a real sense. Nations really have their own temperaments, but the individual can very well rise above the national temperament; one is not necessarily predisposed to it. You must be careful not to identify the individuality of the particular person with the temperament of his whole nation. For example, it would be wrong to identify the individual Russian of today with the temperament of the Russian nation. The latter would be melancholic while the individual Russian of today is inclined to be sanguine.

The quality of the national temperament is expressed in the various languages, so one could certainly say that the language

---

4. Felix Balde is a character in the Mystery Plays.

of one nation is like this, and the language of another nation is like that. It is true to say that the English language is thoroughly phlegmatic and Greek exceptionally sanguine. Such things can be said as indications of real facts. The German language, being two-sided in nature, has very strongly melancholic and also very strongly sanguine characteristics. You can see this when the German language appears in its original form, particularly in the language of philosophy. Let me remind you of the wonderful quality of Fichte's philosophical language or of some passages in Hegel's *Aesthetics*, where you find the fundamental character of German language expressed with unusual clarity. The Italian folk-spirit has a special relationship to air, the French a special connection with fluids, the English and American, especially the English, with the solid earth, the American even with the sub-earthly—that is, with earth magnetism and earth electricity. Then we have the Russian who is connected with the light— that is, with earth's light that rays back from plants. The German folk-spirit is connected with warmth, and you see at once that this has a double character—inner and outer, warmth of the blood and warmth of the atmosphere. Here again you find a polaric character even in the distribution of these elementary conditions. You see this polarity at once—this cleavage in the German nature, which can be found there in everything.

*Question: Should the children know anything about this classification according to temperament?*

RUDOLF STEINER: This is something that must be kept from the children. Much depends on whether the teacher has the right and tactful feeling about what should be kept hidden. The purpose of all these things we have spoken of here is to give the teacher authority. The teacher who doesn't use discretion in what to say cannot be successful.

Students should not be seated according to their attainments, and you will find it advantageous to refuse requests from children to sit together.

*Question: Is there a connection between the temperaments and the choice of foreign languages for the different temperaments of the children?*

RUDOLF STEINER: Theoretically that would be correct, but it would not be advisable to consider it given current conditions. It will never be possible to be guided only by what is right according to the child's disposition; we have to remember also that children must make their way in the world, and we have to give them what they need to do that. If in the near future, for example, it appeared as if a great many German children had no aptitude for learning English, it would not be good to give in to this weakness. Just those who show a weakness of this kind may be the first to need to know English.

*There was a discussion on the task given the previous day: to consider the case of a whole class that, incited by one child, was guilty of very bad behavior; for example, they had been spitting on the ceiling. Some views were expressed on this matter.*

RUDOLF STEINER interjected various remarks: It is a very practical method to wait for something like this to wear out, so that the children stop doing it on their own. You should always be able to distinguish whether something is done out of malice or high spirits.

One thing I would like to say: Even the best teacher will have naughtiness in the class, but if a whole class takes part it is usually the teacher's fault. If it isn't the teacher's fault, you will always find that a group of children are on the teacher's side and will be a support. Only when the teacher has failed will the whole class take part in insubordination.

If there has been any damage, then of course it is proper that it should be corrected, and the children themselves must do this—not by paying for it, but with their own hands. You could use a Sunday, or even two or three Sundays to repair any damage. And remember, humor is also a good method of reducing things to an absurdity, especially minor faults.

I gave you this problem to think on to help you see how to tackle something that occurs when one child incites the others. To demonstrate where the crux of the matter lies, I will tell you a story of something that actually occurred. In a class where things of this kind often happened, and where the teachers could not cope with them, one of the boys between ten and twelve years old went up to the front during the interval between two lessons and said, "Ladies and gentlemen! Aren't you ashamed of always doing things like this, you good-for-nothings? Just remember, you would all remain completely stupid if the teachers didn't teach you anything." This had the most wonderful effect.

We can learn something from this episode: When a large proportion of the class does something like this because of the instigation of one or more of the children, it may very well happen that, also through the influence of a few, order may be restored. If a few children have been instigators there will be others, two or three perhaps, who express disapproval. There are almost always leaders among the children, so the teacher should pick out two or three considered suitable and arrange a conversation with them. The teacher would have to make it clear that behavior of this kind makes teaching impossible, and that they should recognize this and make their influence felt in the class. These children will then have just as much influence as the instigators, and they can make things clear to their classmates. In any situation like this you must consider how the children affect one another.

The most important thing here is that you should evoke feelings that will lead them away from naughtiness. A harsh punishment on the part of the teacher would only cause fear and so on. It would never inspire the children to do better. The teacher must remain as calm as possible and adopt an objective attitude. That does not mean lessening the teacher's own authority. The teacher could certainly be the one to say, "Without your teachers you would learn nothing and remain stupid." But the teacher should allow the correction be carried out by the other children, leaving it to them to make their schoolmates feel ashamed.

We thus appeal to feelings rather than to judgment. But when the whole class is repeatedly against the teacher, then the fault must be looked for in the teacher. Most naughtiness arises because the children are bored and lack a relationship with their teacher.

When a fault is not too serious it can certainly be very good for the teacher to do just what the pupils are doing—to say, for example, when the pupils are grumbling, "Well I can certainly grumble too!" In this way the matter is treated homeopathically, as it were. Homeopathic treatment is excellent for moral education. It's also a good way to divert the children's attention to something else (although I would never appeal to their ambition). In general, however, we seldom have to complain of such misdemeanors. Whenever you allow mischievousness of this kind to be corrected by other children in the class, you work on the feelings to reestablish weakened authority. When another pupil stresses that gratitude must be felt toward the teacher, then the respect for authority will be restored again. It is important to choose the right children; you must know your class and pick those suited to the task.

If I taught a class I could venture to do this. I would try to find the ringleader, whom I would compel to denounce, as much as possible, such conduct, to say as many bad things about it as possible, and I would ignore the fact that it was this student who had done it. I would then bring the matter quickly to a close so that a sense of uncertainty would be left in the minds of the children, and you will come to see that much can be gained from this element of uncertainty. And to make one of the rascals involved describe the incident correctly and objectively will not in any way lead to hypocrisy. I would consider any actual punishment superfluous, even harmful. The essential thing is to arouse a feeling for the objective damage that has been caused and the necessity of correcting it. If teaching time has been lost in dealing with this matter, then it must be made good after school hours, not as a punishment but simply to make up the time lost.

I will now present a problem of a more psychological nature: if you have some rather unhealthy "goody-goodies" in the class—children who try to curry favor in various ways, who have a habit of continually coming to the teacher about this, that, and the other, how would you treat them? Of course you can treat the matter extremely simply. You could say: I am simply not going to bother with them. But then this peculiarity will be turned into other channels: these "good" children will gradually become a harmful element in the class.

# Discussion Six

STUTTGART, AUGUST 27, 1919

*Repetition of yesterday's speech exercises.*

New speech exercises:

> Rateless ration
> roosted roomily
> reason wretched
> ruined Roland
> royalty roster
>
> Proxy prized
> bather broomstick
> polka pushing
> beady basket
> prudent pertness
> bearskin bristled

*One of Lessing's fables was read.*

RUDOLF STEINER: You have to remember that prose can be read in varying tone according to the reader's personality. Also, the title of a fable of this kind is not very important and should not be emphasized particularly.

### The Nightingale and the Peacock

A friendly nightingale found among the singers of the wood enviers galore, but no friend. "Perhaps I shall find one among a different species," she thought, and flew down trustfully to the peacock. "Beautiful Peacock, I admire you very much." "I you, too, dear Nightingale." "Then let us be friends," the nightingale continued, "we ought not to be envious of each other. You are as pleasing to the eye as I am to the ear." The nightingale and the peacock became friends.

Kneller and Pope were better friends than were Pope and Addison. [1]

RUDOLF STEINER: Now there is an educational matter I would like to talk over with you. I want to point out that you should never spoil the contents of a "passage" by first reading it aloud yourself, or reading it through with your students, and then pedantically explaining it, because this will destroy the powers of feeling and perception in the children. A teacher with insight will not work this way, but will feel that hearing a bit of prose or poetry should produce a sense of contentment in the soul—a satisfaction should arise from hearing a passage of prose or poetry read. The children will then fully understand every shade of meaning. Within their feelings, in any case, they will instinctively understand what the poem contains. It is unnecessary to go into subtleties or to make learned comments about a poem or prose passage, but through your teaching the children should rise to a complete understanding of it through feelings. Hence you should always try to leave the

---

1. Rudolf Steiner jokingly added an alternate example: France and Italy are better friends than Italy and England. Thus you see that the fable can be applied in the most varying ways.

actual reading of a piece until last, first dealing with everything you can give the children to help them understand it. If
you prepare for the reading as well as you can ahead of time,
then you will not work like a pedant, but help make the whole
piece clear and understandable, and thus enhance the children's enjoyment and satisfaction.

I would therefore take something like the following with the
children (but you would have to work it out in greater detail). I
would say: "Now look, boys and girls, you have certainly seen
some dogs at some time or other in your life. If any of you have
never seen a dog then you must have been hiding in some dark
corner! And you must have noticed that not all dogs are alike.
They are very, very different from one another. There are tiny
little dogs, small dogs, larger dogs, and great, big dogs. You
have probably always been afraid of the very large dogs; but
you have not been afraid of the tiny little dogs—or maybe you
have, because sometimes they bite people's calves.

"Now today we will look at some of these dogs. You have
probably often seen a meat cart in the streets pulled by a
butcher's dog. If you have looked carefully, you have probably
noticed that the rest of the time this dog sits in front of the
butcher's stall and makes sure no one steals the meat. If anyone
comes who isn't allowed and takes the meat, the dog must bite
that person, or at least bark. Now, you see a butcher's dog cannot be a tiny little animal; no, he must be a big dog. You will
also notice that small dogs are never harnessed to a butcher's
cart, nor do they watch a butcher's stall.

"You can compare a butcher's dog with a person who has to
guard something. You can often compare animals with people.
Animals have to do things through instinct, and people must
often do the same things because it is their duty. People and
animals have to do similar things and therefore they can be
compared.

"Suppose a man has to guard something just like a butcher's dog does at the meat stall; the man will form a certain habit. If someone comes and tries to steal something, he will take hold of him by the hair. Yes, when someone is doing something wrong— you take hold of such a person 'by the comb.' But a person has hair, not a real comb. You pull the hair, and that hurts, so the person doesn't try to get away; that is why you do it. You don't say this kind of thing point blank. If you said straight out, 'I will pull your hair,' it wouldn't be as much fun. There must always be a little fun in life, so you say that you take someone 'by the comb.' A person has hair, and is sometimes insolent; a rooster is almost always insolent, and has a comb; that's why you say, 'I'll take you by the comb.' You can imagine that if, for example, another insolent creature came along, wanting to take a piece of meat out of the stall, the butcher's dog might say, 'I'll take you by the comb!' Then you would have made a very good comparison between a person and a dog.

"Now you know, children, there are also other dogs, small dogs, who are mostly lazy creatures; they are miserably lazy. They lie on cushions or sometimes even on laps. Basically, they are idle fellows. They are 'cushion-dogs,' those 'lapdogs.' They are not as useful as the butcher's dog. The butcher's dog is of some service; the lapdogs, they only play; they are basically useless. But if anyone does anything wrong, the butcher's dog will take that person by the comb—the dog will seize that person and give a thorough shaking. This is of some use, because the other creature will not be able to steal the meat.

"The lapdog doesn't do anything useful like that, but only yaps, yaps at everybody; and especially when big dogs come along, the little lapdog rushes out and yaps and yaps and yaps. But their bark is worse than their bite; that is what the proverb says and that is what the large dogs think as they pass by. You can also see how large dogs go by very calmly; they let the little yappers yap, and think to themselves: Yapping dogs don't bite, they are not brave, they are cowardly. But a butcher's dog must always have courage. The lapdogs run after the big dog and yap, but if the butcher's dog turns round and looks at them, they immediately run away. So you see these little dogs are certainly lazy; they only do what is unnecessary and they are good for nothing. They are like certain people whom we should not listen to, even though they very often yap at us.

"These lapdogs are very small, the butcher's dog is large. But there are other dogs in between—not as big as the butcher's dog, but larger than the lapdog. Among the medium-sized dogs is the sheep-dog. The sheep-dog has to guard the sheep. In many districts it is a more difficult job than here. In many places—in Russia, for example—there are wolves, and the dog has to keep the wolves or any other animals away from the sheep; and so the sheepdog has gotten into the habit of continually running round the flock. In our country too it is good to have dogs who run round the flock all the time, because the shepherd is often asleep, and any evil-minded creature could come and steal some of the flock. So the sheepdog runs round and guards the flock. Even when there are no wolves, it is good for the sheepdog to run round and guard the flock; and sometimes the sheepdog guards the shepherd, as well, who is then awakened. It might even happen that a shepherd could be stolen while asleep!

"Thus the shepherd's dog, the sheepdog, is of service; the sheepdog is a useful animal and can be compared with people who have found their proper work in life, people who are not useless like the idlers, the lapdogs. Yes, in human life too there is this difference between those who are like sheepdogs and those who are like butcher's dogs. They are both useful, although the latter, like the butcher's dog, are at times rather rough. Sometimes they say exactly the right thing in a few words and straight to the point, to guard something, to ward off an enemy. You can make a comparison with the sheepdogs also; they are like people who work quietly, waiting calmly until difficulties are upon them. The sheepdog runs round and round for a long time; he has nothing to do, but he must always be prepared for action, so that when the wolf or another enemy appears the sheepdog will be strong and courageous and well prepared to attack at the right moment. There are also people who have the duty to watch and wait until they are called on to fulfil some task. They must not allow themselves to be harassed by petty things in life, but always have to be ready for the moment when they must act, and act correctly."

This is how I would speak to children, choosing some particular example from the animal world and leading their thoughts to analogies between animals and people. After speaking somewhat in this way you can read aloud the following passage, and when you have read it explanations will be unnecessary. If you were to give the children this little story first without any explanation they would not be fully prepared, because their perceptions and feelings would not be directed to what it contains. If on the other hand you do not explain until afterward, you would pedantically pull the passage apart, and so they would not be able to read it properly either.

## The Sheepdog

One evening an old sheepdog who was a faithful keeper of the master's sheep was on the way home. As he went down the street, some little lapdogs yapped at him. He trotted on without looking around. When he came to the meat stall, a butcher's dog asked him how he could stand such constant barking and why he didn't take one of them by the scruff of the neck. "I won't," said the herdsman's dog, "none of them are worrying me or biting me; I must save my teeth for the wolves."

You do not need to say another word to the children. The preparation must come first so that they understand what is read.

Another time you can say to the children, "My dear children! You have often gone for a walk; you have certainly gone for a walk in a meadow, in the fields, also in woods, and sometimes on the edge of the woods where the trees and meadow meet. While you walk in the wood you are right in the shade, but when you are on the edge of the woods the Sun can still shine very brightly on one side. When you find a meadow that borders the woods, you should stand quietly and watch, and see how the flowers grow. It's always good when during your walks you look especially for the places where the trees meet the meadow, because then you can always be looking for something, sometimes in the woods, and sometimes in the meadow; you can continually notice afresh how the grass grows, and how the plants and the flowers grow in the grass.

"But you know, it is especially beautiful and lovely—a real delight—when you can go, not just through woods and fields, but somewhere where the meadows lie among mountains and valleys. Here you'll find much more interesting things than in the meadows, which often get too much sun. Valley meadows that are protected by the mountains have very beautiful flowers, which we can often find among the moss growing in great abundance in these valley meadows. Violets especially are always found with moss growing near them."

Then you can continue talking to the children about moss and violets, perhaps calling on a child to describe a violet and another to talk about moss. And when it is the right season you might even bring some violets and moss to school with you, because they can be gathered at the same time of year.

Then you could continue, "But look, dear children, if you have a valley of this kind near your home, maybe you could go there one day and only see moss. Then a week later you could go there again. What would you see this time? Violets growing in the moss! Yes, they have just appeared; when you were there before, they were hidden in the moss. Remember this, and next year when you go there you can have even greater pleasure, because now you think to yourselves: Last spring there weren't any violets showing here yet, we didn't see one. And then you try to separate the moss with your fingers. Ah! A violet! There it is!

"In nature, my dear children, it is often just as it is with people. There, too, much is often hidden that is good, much that is beautiful. Many people are not noticed because the good in them is concealed, it has not yet been found. You must try to awaken the feeling that will enable you to find the good people in the crowd.

"Yes, dear children, and there is still another way that you can compare human life with nature. Think of a really good person whom you know, and you will always find that person's words to be honest and good. Now some people are modest and others are proud and arrogant. Modest people don't attract much attention, but the pushy ones always like to be noticed.

"Now a violet is certainly very beautiful, but when you look at this violet and see how it stretches up its lovely little petals, you cannot fail to see that the violet wants to be noticed, it wants to be looked at. So I could not compare the violet with a modest little child who keeps in the corner out of the way. You could only compare it with a child who is really very anxious to be seen. You will say: That may be, but it doesn't show itself when it's hidden in the moss, does it? Yes, but look; when you see how the violet comes out among its leaves and then again how the whole plant creeps out of the moss, it is just as though the violet not only wanted people to see it and smell it, but to search for it as well. 'Yes, yes! Here I am, here I am but you have to look for me!' And so the violet is like a person who is certainly not modest but rather a sly rascal."

It is good to discuss comparisons of this kind with the children, and to show them analogies between nature and human beings so that everything around them becomes alive.

You should have these talks with the children ahead of time, so they can enjoy the reading when it comes. *After* the reading no more explanations of any kind should be given. You will agree it would not make sense if I were now to begin giving you a lecture in Chinese. You would say, "That is senseless, because we never learned Chinese." But if you all knew Chinese when I gave my lecture, you would find it extremely dull if afterwards I wanted to explain it all to you. You should have the same feeling about a piece of reading and do everything you can to make it enjoyable.

Talks such as these about modesty and conceit in people—and affectation, as well—can be developed in greater detail than we have done today, and you must let the children take a lively share. Then you can read them the following poem:

What's gleaming in the sunshine though fast asleep?
Oh, those are tiny violets that bloom in valley deep.
Bloom quite hidden in moss-covered ground,
So that we children no violets have found.

And what's this little head that stretches silent there?
What whispers in the moss so still and quiet here?
"Search and you will find me, search for me still!"
"Wait, violet, wait, and find you we will!"
                              —Hofmann von Fallersleben

When you teach children a poem in this way, they can enter its every nuance, and it will be unnecessary to spoil the impression with commentary and pedantry afterward. This is the method I want to recommend to you with regard to your treatment of selections for reading, because it will give you the opportunity to talk over many things that belong in your teaching, and further, the children will have a real feeling of satisfaction when such passages are read. This then is what I wish to lay upon your hearts about reading.

We will now continue our discussion on the treatment of individual children. Yesterday I asked you to think over how to treat "virtuous," "good" children (the goody-goodies), who assert themselves but are not helpful to the rest of the class.

*Various contributions were presented.*

RUDOLF STEINER: I have presented this particular problem because it is difficult to discriminate between the harmful, self-righteous children and those who can play a useful role. You must notice whether you are dealing with those who really have a contribution to make later. That is their nature. They are "useful" goody-goodies, but a bit of a nuisance!

In such a case you could relate the story of how the donkey got big ears. You can even use stronger measures with some of these goody-goody children, but you should *not* expose them to the class and thus reflect shame on them. That would be going too far. But you can give such a forward child exceptionally difficult tasks, with rod exercises for example, and let the facts speak for themselves; in this way, such children see that they cannot perform, and they have to tell the teacher so. From this it can become apparent whether their boasting was justified.

*Other teachers made further remarks.*

RUDOLF STEINER: The essentials of the problem have been presented in this discussion. First you must very carefully ascertain the worthiness of the self-assertiveness of the pupils who are more gifted and therefore more capable. You must not allow their greater talent to develop into ambitious egoism, but help them to use their gifts to help the other children. You can get the smart children like this to do something with their special powers that will help the others, so that they do not work just for themselves, but for the other children as well. If they are better at arithmetic, have them do the problem first, and let the others *learn from them.* Their greater ability is channeled properly when they hear from the teacher the consequence of a line of thought that could be expressed in this way: John is a good boy. Look how much he can do. Such people are a great help to others, and I'm very pleased with all of you that you learned so much from John."

So you begin by praising one child and end by praising them all! When you have outstanding talent of this kind and have singled out these very self-possessed children (of whom there are always some), you will almost always find that you can deal most effectively with them by combining two methods. First, you must speak to them, not in front of the class, but in private so that they will realize that you see through them. You must very emphatically say, "You are doing this or doing that," and then you characterize their qualities. In such a case you must then strike a personal note: "All right, you can go on doing it, you can do it over and over again. But do you think I like it? Do you think that you are pleasing me? No, I don't like it at all; I find it very disagreeable." This is how you should speak to them—as I say, not in front of the class, but in private. That is the first thing. You must make it very clear that you see through the student.

The second thing is this: you should give such children tasks beyond their powers and try to make it clear to them why they have to solve these problems that are too difficult for them; it is because they want to assert themselves. It is harder for such children to battle this propensity than to solve problems that are beyond them. But it is more disagreeable for them to do these tasks, so they will try to become less conceited, and we must tell them that they have been given these tasks because of their assertiveness. But if they can overcome their desire to be noticed, then they will not get anything different from the rest of the class.

But you can do both of these things together in the case of such pupils, whether boys or girls, you can combine the two methods—letting them know that you see through them and telling them why they get especially difficult tasks. By using these two methods together you will accomplish much. After some time, if you apply these methods, you will see that you have cured your students.

We still have many more difficult problems to solve in these discussions. But for tomorrow I would like to give you a similar problem connected with the last one, and yet a bit different; and in our treatment of this, eurythmy will be considered. Forgive me for placing this before you, but it belongs to the area of teaching. What should you do when, among your students, a foolish kind of adoration arises for the teacher. Does everyone know what I mean by "adoration?" It is when a boy idolizes a female teacher or the other way round, when a girl idolizes a male teacher, or when a girl adores a female teacher or a boy a male teacher. All these different varieties exist. Any real manifestation of this foolish adoration can be very disturbing to the pursuit of your work; please think about how it should be treated.

It must of course take such a serious form that your lessons are actually disturbed by it. Of course I do not mean genuine respect and sincere regard, neither do I mean proper affection and love for a female or male teacher, but just a kind of unhealthy adoration that disturbs your teaching, which is frequently found in classes.

# Discussion Seven

STUTTGART, AUGUST 28, 1919

Today we will try an exercise in which we have to hold the breath somewhat longer. Speech exercise:

> Fulfilling goes
> through hoping
> goes through longing
> through willing
> willing flows
> in wavering
> wails in quavering
> waves veiling
> waving breathing
> in freedom
> freedom winning
> kindling

You can only achieve what is intended by dividing the lines properly. Then you will bring the proper rhythm to your breath. The object of this exercise is to do gymnastics with the voice in order to regulate the breath.

In words like *fulfilling* and *willing*, both "l's" must be pronounced. You shouldn't put an "h" into the first "l", but the two "l's" must be sounded one after the other.

You must also try to avoid speaking with a rasping voice, and develop instead tone in your voice, bringing it up from deeper in your chest, to give full value to the vowels. (All Austrians have tinny voices!)

Before each of the above lines the breath should be consciously brought into order. The words that appear together also belong together when you *read*.

You know that we usually do the following speech exercises also:

> *Barbara sass stracks am Abhang*
> or:  *Barbara sass nah am abhang*
> or:  *Abraham a Sancta Clara kam an*[1]

### The Steed and the Bull.

An impudent boy came flying along on a fiery steed. A wild bull called out to the horse, "Shame on you! I would not be governed by a lad!" "But I would," replied the horse, "for what kind of honor would it bring me to throw the boy off?"

*They all read the fable aloud.*

RUDOLF STEINER: After hearing this fable so often you will certainly sense that it is written in the particular style of fables and many other writings of the eighteenth century. You get the feeling that they didn't quite finish, just as other things were not fully completed then.

*Rudolf Steiner read the fable aloud again.*

---

1. The entire verse: "*Barbara sass nah am Abhang, / Sprach gar sangbar—zaghaft langsam; / Mannhaft kam alsdann am Waldrand / Abraham a Sancta Clara!*" is from material given by Julius Hey in *Die Kunst der Sprache*, Mainz-Leipzig, 1914. Rudolf Steiner found that these sound-sequences could be used and also mentioned the exercise of Hey's for *E* (*eh*). While Hey's exercises have a certain meaning, the exercises given by Steiner come purely from the element of sound.

RUDOLF STEINER: Now, in the twentieth century the fable would be continued something like this: "That may be the honor of bulls! And if I were to seek honor by stubbornly standing still, that would not be a horse's honor but a mule's honor!" That is how it would be written in these days. Then the children would notice immediately that there are three kinds of honor; the honor of a bull, the honor of a horse, and the honor of a mule. The bull throws the boy, the horse carries him quietly along because that is chivalrous, the mule stubbornly stands still because that is the mule's idea of honor.

Today I would like to give you some material for tomorrow's discussion on the subject of your lessons, since we will then consider particularly the seven-to-fourteen-year-old children.[2]

So we will now speak of certain things that can guide you, and after I have presented this introduction, you will only need an ordinary reference book to amplify the various facts we have spoken of in our discussions. Today we will consider not so much how to acquire the actual subject matter of our work, but rather how to cherish and cultivate within ourselves the *spirit of an education that contains the future within it.* You will see that what we discuss today focuses on the work in the oldest classes.[3]

I would therefore like to discuss what relates to the history of European civilization from the eleventh to the seventeenth century. You must always remember that teaching history to children should always contain a subjective element, and this is also true, more or less, when you work with adults. It is easy enough to say that people should not bring opinions and subjective ideas into history. You might make this a rule, but it

---

2. *Practical Advice to Teachers,* lecture 8.
3. The Waldorf School began with grades 1–8 only. The oldest children in the school were thus fourteen to fifteen years of age.

cannot be adhered to. Take aspect of history in any country of the world; you will either have to arrange the facts in groups for yourself, or you will find them already thus assembled by others in the case of less recent history.

If, for example, you want to describe the spirit of the old Germanic peoples, you will turn to the *Germania* of Tacitus. But Tacitus was a person of very subjective thought; the facts he presents were clearly arranged in groups. You can only hope to succeed in your task by marshalling the facts in your own personal way, or else by using what others have done in a similar way before you. You can find examples, from literature for example, to substantiate what I have said.

Treitschke wrote *German History of the Nineteenth Century* in several volumes; it delighted Herman Grimm, who was also a competent judge, but it horrified many adherents of the entente. But when you read Treitschke you will feel immediately that his excellence is due to the very subjective coloring of his grouping of facts. In history the important thing is the ability to form a judgment of the underlying forces and powers at work. But you must realize that the judgment of one is more mature, that of another less so, and the latter should not pass any judgment at all because nothing has been understood about the underlying forces. The former, just because an independent judgment has been formed, will very well describe the actual course of history.

Herman Grimm portrayed Frederick the Great, and Macaulay also portrayed him, but Macaulay's picture is completely different. Grimm even composed his article as a kind of critique of Macaulay's article, and speaking from his perspective he said, "Macaulay's picture of Frederick the Great is the grotesque face of an English lord with snuff on his nose!" The only difference is that Grimm is a nineteenth-century German and Macaulay a nineteenth-century Englishman. And any third person passing judgment on both would really be very narrow-minded if one were found to be true and the other false.

You might as well choose examples even more drastic. Many of you know the description of Martin Luther in the ordinary history books. If one day you try the experiment of reading it in the Catholic history books, you will get to know a Martin Luther whom you never knew before! But when you have read it you will find it difficult to say that the difference is anything but different viewpoints. Now it is just such points of view arising from nation or creed that must be overcome by future teachers. Because of this we must earnestly work so that teachers are broad-minded, so that the point will be reached of having a broad-minded philosophy of life. Such a mental attitude gives you a free and wide view of historical facts, and a skillful arranging of these facts will enable you to convey to your pupils the secrets of human evolution.

Now, when you want to give the children some idea of cultural history from the eleventh to the seventeenth centuries, you would first have to describe what led up to the Crusades. You would describe the course of the first, second, and third crusades, and how they gradually stagnated, failing to achieve what they should have. You would describe the spirit of asceticism that spread through much of Europe at the time—how everywhere, through the secularization of the church (or in any case in connection with *this* secularization), there arose individuals such as Bernard of Clairvaux, natures full of inner piety, such piety that it gave the impression to others that they were miracleworkers. From reference books you could try to become acquainted with biographies of people of this kind and then bring them to life for your pupils; you could try to conjure before them the living spirit that inspired those great expeditions to the East—because they were powerful in the views of the time. You would have to describe how these expeditions came to be through Peter of Amiens and Walter the Penniless, followed by the expedition of Godfrey of Bouillon and others.

Then you could relate how these Crusades set out toward the East and how enormous numbers of people perished, often before they reached their destination. You can certainly describe to boys and girls of thirteen to fifteen how these expeditions were composed, how they set out without any organization and made their way toward the East, and how many perished because of unfavorable conditions, and having to force their way through foreign countries and peoples.

You will then have to describe how those who reached the East had a certain degree of success at first. You can speak of what Godfrey of Bouillon accomplished, but you will also have to show the contrast that arose between the Crusaders of the later Crusades and Greek policy—how the Greeks became jealous of what the Crusaders were doing, feeling that the Crusaders' goals were contrary to what the Greeks themselves were planning to do in the East; how fundamentally the Greeks, as much as the Crusaders, wanted to absorb the interests of the East into their own sphere of interests. Paint a graphic picture of how the goals of the Crusaders roused the Greeks' opposition.

Then I suggest that you describe how the crusading armies in the East, instead of taking up arms against the Eastern peoples in western Asia, began to fight among themselves; and how the European peoples themselves, especially the Franks and their neighbors, began to quarrel about their claims to conquests and even took up arms against each other. The Crusades originated in fiery enthusiasm, but the spirit of inner discord seized those who took part in them; furthermore, antagonism arose between the Crusaders and the Greeks.

In addition to all this, at the very time of the Crusades we find opposition between church and state, and this became more and more evident. It may also be necessary to acquaint the children with something that is true, although in all its essential points it is veiled by the bias of historical writers. Godfrey of Bouillon, the leader of the first Crusade, really intended to conquer Jerusalem in order to balance the influence of Rome. He and his companions did not say this openly to the others, but in their hearts they carried the battle cry, "Jerusalem versus Rome!" They said among themselves, "Let us exalt Jerusalem so that it may become the center of Christianity, so that Rome no longer holds that position." This, the underlying motive of the first Crusaders, can be conveyed to the children tactfully, and it is important to do so.

Those were great tasks that the Crusaders undertook, and great too were the tasks that gradually arose from the circumstances themselves. Little by little it came to be that the Crusaders were not great enough to bear the burden of such tasks without harm to themselves. And so it happened that, at the time of the fiercest battles, licentiousness and immorality gradually broke out among the Crusaders.

You can find these facts in any history book, and they serve to illustrate the general course of events. You will notice that in my arrangement of facts today, I am actually describing them without bias, and I will try also to describe in a purely historical way what took place in Europe from the eleventh to the seventeenth century.

It is often possible to make history clear through hypothesis, so let's suppose that the Franks had conquered Syria and had established a Frankish dominion there—that they had reached an understanding with the Greeks, had left room for them, and had relinquished to them the rule of the more western portion of Asia Minor. Then the ancient traditions of the Greeks would have been fulfilled and North Africa would have become Greek. A counterbalance to subsequent events would have thus been established. The Greeks would have held sway in North

Africa, the Franks in Syria. Then they wouldn't have quarrelled with each other, and thus they wouldn't have forfeited their dominions, and the invasions of the worst Eastern peoples—the Mongols, the Mamelukes, and Turkish Ottoman—would have been prevented. Because of the immorality of the Crusaders, and inevitably their inability to rise to their tasks, the Mongols, Mamelukes, and Ottomans overran the very regions that the Crusaders were attempting to "Europeanize." And so we see how the reaction toward the great enthusiasm that led to the Crusades, spread over vast regions, is counterattacked from the other side. We see the Moslem-Mongolian advance, which set up military tyrants, and which for a long time remained the terror of Europe and cast a dark shadow over the history of the Crusades.

You see, by describing such things and acquiring the necessary pictorial descriptions from reference books, you can awaken in the children themselves pictures of the progress of civilization—pictures that will live on in them. And that is the important thing—that the children be given these pictures. They will initially be conjured in their minds through your graphic descriptions. If you can then show them some works of art, notable paintings from this period, you will find this supports what you say.

Thus, you will make it clear to the children what happened during the Crusades, and enable them to make their own mental pictures of these events. You have shown them the dark side of the picture, the terror caused by the Mongolians and Moslems, and now it will be well to add the other side, the good things that developed.

Describe vividly to the children how the pilgrims who had migrated east, came to understand many new things there. Agriculture, for example, was at that time very backward in Europe. In the East it was possible for these Western pilgrims to learn a much better way of farming their land. The pilgrims who reached the East and afterward returned to Europe (and many did return), brought with them a skilled knowledge of agricultural methods, which raised the standard of agricultural production considerably. The Europeans owed this to the experience that the pilgrims brought back with them.

You must describe this to the children so graphically that they actually see it there before them—how the wheat and other cereals flourished less before the Crusades, how they were smaller, more sparse, the ears less full, and how after the Crusades they were much fuller. Describe all this in *pictures!* Then you can also tell how the pilgrims really came to understand industries found in the East at the time, and still unknown in Europe. The West was in many ways more backward than the East. What grew and flourished in such a fine way in the industrial activity of the Italian towns and other places further north, was all due to the Crusades; we also have to thank them for a new artistic impulse. Thus you can call on pictures of the cultural and spiritual progress of that time.

There is something else you can describe to the children: you can say to them, "You see, children, that was when the Europeans came to know the Greeks; they had fallen away from Rome in the first thousand years after Christ, but had remained Christians. All over the West people believed that no one could be a Christian without viewing the Pope as the head of the church." Now explain to the children how the Crusaders, to their astonishment and edification, learned that there were other Christians who did not acknowledge the Roman Pope. This freeing of the spiritual side of Christianity from the temporal church organization was something very new at the time. This is something you can explain to the children.

Then you can tell them that even among the Moslems, who could scarcely have been called very pleasant denizens of the world, there were also noble, generous, and brave people. And so the pilgrims came to know people who could be brave and generous without being Christians; thus a person could even be good and brave without being a Christian. For the Europeans of that time this was a great lesson that the Crusaders brought with them when they returned to Europe. During their stay in the East they gained many things that they brought back to Europe to further its spiritual progress.

You can then continue, "Just imagine, children, there was a time when the Europeans had no cotton cloth, they did not even have a word for it; they had no muslin—that too is an Eastern word; they could not lie down or laze about on a sofa, for sofas and the word for them were brought back by the Crusaders. They had no mattresses either. *Mattress* is also an Asian word. The *bazaar* also belongs to the East, and this suggests immediately an entirely new view of the public display of goods, and it initiated large scale exhibitions of goods. Bazaars (of an Eastern kind) were very common in the East, but there was nothing of the kind in Europe before the Europeans went on their Crusades. Even the word *magazine* [the word for "storeroom" in German] bound up though it now is with our trade life, was not originally European; the use of great warehouses to meet the growth of trade is something that the Europeans learned from the Asians.

"Just imagine," you can say to the children, "how restricted life was in Europe; they hadn't even any warehouses. The word *arsenal* too has the same origin. But now look; there is something else that the Europeans learned from the East and that is expressed in the word *tariff.* Until the thirteenth century the European peoples knew very little about tax-paying. But payment of taxes according to a tariff, the payment of all kinds of duties, was not introduced into Europe until the Crusaders learned about it from the Asians.

"Thus you see that a great number of things were changed in Europe due to the Crusades. Not much of what the Crusaders intended to do was realized, but other things were brought about, and transformations of all kinds occurred in Europe as a result of what was learned in the East. And further, this was all connected with what they observed of the Eastern political life. Political life—the state as such—developed much earlier in the East than in Europe. Before the Crusades the forms of government in Europe were much freer than they were afterward. Because of the Crusades it also happened that wide areas were grouped together as political units."

Always assuming that the children are of the age I indicated, you can now say to them, "You have already learned in your history lessons that in former times the Romans became rulers over many lands. When they were extending their dominions, at the beginning of the Christian era, Europe was very poor and becoming even poorer. What was the cause of this increasing poverty? The people had to hand over their money to others. Central Europe will become poor again today because it must also hand over its money to others. At that time the Europeans had to give up their money to the Asiatics; the bulk of their money went to the borders of the Roman Empire. Due to this, barter became more and more the custom, and this is something that might happen again, sad though it would be, unless people rouse themselves to seek the spirit. Nevertheless, amid this poverty the ascetic, devotional spirit of the Crusades evolved.

"Through the Crusades, therefore, in faraway Asia, Europeans learned to know all kinds of things—industrial production, agriculture, and so on. In this way, they could again produce things that the Asians could buy from them. Money traveled back again. Europe became increasingly rich during the Crusades. This growth of wealth in Europe occurred through the increase in its own productions; that is a further result of the

Crusades. The Crusades are indeed migrations of peoples to Asia, and when the Crusaders returned to Europe they brought with them a certain ability. It was due only to this ability and skill that Florence, Italy arose and became what it did, and also due to this, such figures as Dante and others emerged."

You see how necessary it is to allow impulses of this kind to permeate your history lessons. When it is said today that more should be taught about the history of civilizations, people think they should give dry descriptions of how one thing arises from another. But even in these lower classes, history should be described by a teacher who really lives in the subject, so that through the pictures created for the children, this period of history will live again before them. You can conjure the picture of a poverty-stricken Europe, with acres of poor and sparsely sown crops, where there were no towns—only meager farms in poor condition. Nevertheless, an enthusiasm for the Crusades arises out of this same poor Europe. But then you will have to tell them how the people found this task beyond their powers and they began to quarrel and fall into evil ways, and even when they were back in Europe discord and dissension arose again. The real purpose of the Crusades was not achieved; on the contrary, the ground was prepared for the Moslems. But the Europeans learned many things in the East: how towns—flourishing towns—arise, and in the towns a rich spiritual life and culture; agriculture improved and the fields became more fertile, the industries flourished, and a spiritual life and culture arose.

You will try to present all this to the children in graphic pictures and explain to them that, before the Crusades, people did not lounge on sofas! There was no bourgeois life at that time with sofas in the best parlors and all the rest of it. Try to make all these historical pictures *live* for the children, and then you will give them a truer kind of history. Show how Europe became so poor that people had to resort to bartering goods, and then it became rich again because of what people learned in the East. This will bring life into your history lessons!

One is often asked these days what history books to read—which historian is best? The reply can only be that, in the end, each one is the best and the worst; it really makes no difference which historical author you choose. Do not read what is written *in* the lines, but read *between* the lines. Try to allow yourselves to be inspired so that, through your own intuitive sense, you can learn to know the true course of events. Try to acquire a feeling for how a true history should be written. You will recognize from the style and manner of writing which historian has found the truth and which has not.

You can find many things in Ranke.[4] But what we are trying to cultivate here is the spirit of truth and reality, and when you read Ranke in the light of this spirit of truth, you find that he is very painstaking but that his descriptions of characters reduce them to mere shadows; you feel as though you could pass through them, because they have no substance—they are not flesh and blood, and you might well say that you don't want history to be a series of mere phantasms.

*One of the teachers recommended Lamprecht.*[5]

Rudolf Steiner: Yes, but in him you have the feeling that he does not describe people, but figures of colored cardboard—except that he paints them with the most vivid colors possible. They are not human beings, but merely colored cardboard.

---

4. Leopold von Ranke (1795–1886), German historian and founder of the modern school of history. He championed so-called "objective" writing based on source material instead of legend and tradition.
5. Karl Lamprecht (1856–1915) wrote a German history in nineteen volumes.

Now Treitschke on the other hand is admittedly biased, but his personalities do really stand on their two feet![6] He places people on their feet, and they are flesh and blood—not cardboard figures like those of Lamprecht, nor are they mere shadowy pictures as with Ranke. Unfortunately Treitschke's history only covers the nineteenth century.

But, to get a feeling for truly good historical writing, you should read Tacitus.[7] When you read Tacitus, everything is absolutely alive. When you study the way Tacitus portrays a certain epoch of history—describing the people as individuals or in groups—and allow all of this to affect your own sense of reality, it exists for you as real as life itself! Beginning with Tacitus, try to discover how to describe other periods as well.

Of course you can't read what is out of date, otherwise the fiery Rotteck would always be very good.[8] But he is dated, not merely because of the facts, but in his whole outlook; he considers as gospel the political constitution of the Baden of his time, as well as liberalism. He even applies them to Persian, Egyptian, and Greek life, but he always writes with such fire that one cannot help wishing there were many historians like Rotteck today.

If, however, you study the current books on history (with a sharp eye for what is often *left out*), you will gain the capacity to give children *living pictures of the process of human progress* from the eleventh to the seventeenth centuries. And, for your

6. Heinrich von Treitschke (1834–1896), German historian and publicist. Considered the successor to Ranke as Prussian historian, he advocated authoritarian "power politics" (i.e., German unity through force), favored colonial expansion, and promoted anti-British sentiment in Germany.
7. Cornelius Tacitus (A.D. 56–120; not to be confused with Tacitus, the Roman emperor from A.D. 275 to 276), Roman orator, politician, and historian. His main work was *Historiae*.
8. Karl von Rotteck (1775–1840) wrote numerous volumes on national and world history.

part, you can omit much that is said in these histories about Frederick Barbarossa, Richard Coeur de Leon, or Frederick II. Much of this is interesting but not particularly significant for real knowledge of history. It is far more important to communicate to the children the great *impulses* at work in history.

. . . . . .

We can continue now to the question of how to treat a class where several boys and girls have developed a foolish kind of adoration for the male or female teacher.

Idolization of this kind is not really unhealthy until the age of twelve to fourteen, when the problem becomes more serious. Before fourteen it is especially important not to take these things too seriously and to remember that they often disappear again very quickly.

*Various suggestions made by those present.*

RUDOLF STEINER: I would consider that exposing the children to ridicule in front of the class is very much a two-edged sword, because the effect lasts too long, and the child will lose a connection with the class. If you ridicule children it is very difficult for them to regain the proper relationship with the rest of the class. The result is usually that the children succeed in being removed from the school.

*Prayer was mentioned, along with other possible ways of helping these children.*

RUDOLF STEINER: You are quite right!

*It was suggested that one might speak to the child and attempt to divert such affection.*

RUDOLF STEINER: The principle of diverting the devotion and capacity for enthusiasm into other channels is proper—except that you will not gain much by talking with such children, because that is exactly what they want. Precisely because this foolish adoration arises much more from feelings—and even passions—than from thinking, it would be extremely difficult to work against it effectively by being with the child frequently. It is certainly true that unhealthy feelings of this kind are due to the qualities of enthusiasm and devotion having taken the wrong path—enthusiasm in the gifted children and devotion in the less gifted. The whole thing is not very important *in itself*, but it will have repercussions in the way the children participate in the lessons, and this is the more serious aspect. When all of the children are affected by this foolish adoration, it is not so serious and will not last long; it will soon disappear. The class gets ideas that do not materialize; this leads to disappointment, and then the thing dies naturally. In this case it could be very good to tell a humorous story to the whole class. It only becomes detrimental when groups of children yield to this unwholesome idolization.

It became necessary to think this matter over thoroughly, because it can play a role in the entire life of the school. Affectionate attachment is not so bad in itself, but it weakens the children when it becomes unhealthy. The children become listless and lethargic. In some cases it can lead to serious conditions of weakness in the children. It is a very subtle and delicate matter, because the treatment *could* result in turning the children's feelings toward the exact opposite—into hatred. In some cases it could be very good to say, "You look too warm. Perhaps you should go outside for five minutes.

In any case, this problem should be handled individually and each child treated individually. You should try anything that common sense tells you may help. There is one thing however that you should be extremely careful about—that such children do not get the idea that you notice their adoration. You really have to acquire the art of making them think you are unaware of it. Even when you take steps to cure them, the children should think you are merely acting normal.

Let's suppose that several children have this foolish feeling for a man who has four, five, maybe six children of his own. In this case he has the simplest remedy; he can invite the "adoring" children to go for a walk with him and bring his own children along. This would be a very good remedy. But the children should not know why they were invited. You should use concrete things like this.

In a situation like this, it's most important that you yourself act correctly, not treating those children who idolize you any differently than the others. When you remain unaffected by such foolish behavior, it disappears after awhile. It becomes serious, however, when a certain antipathy replaces adoration. This can be minimized by ignoring it. Don't let the children know you have noticed anything, because if you call them on it or ridicule them in front of the class, the hatred will be that much greater. If you tell a story it must appear as though you would have told it anyway, otherwise certain antipathy will certainly arise afterward as a result; that can't be avoided. But when you work with the same class for several years you will be able to restore a normal sympathy over time.

You cannot prevent another consequence, either, because when this foolish adoration assumes a serious form, the children will be somewhat weakened by it. When it is finished, you must help them to get over this weakness. This will indeed be the best therapy that you can apply. You can make use of all the other remedies—sending the children out for five minutes, taking them for walks, and so on, but your attitude must always be to ignore the whole matter in a healthy way. The child will be somewhat weakened, and afterward the teacher will be able to help the child through love and affection. If the matter were to become very serious, the teacher, because of being the object of adoration, could not do much; such a teacher would then have to seek the advice and help of others.

Tomorrow's subject has to do with actual teaching rather than educational principles as such. Will each of you imagine that several children in your class are not doing very well in one subject or another—for example, arithmetic, languages, natural history, gymnastics, or eurythmy. How, through special treatment of the children's human capacities, would you try to meet a misfortune of this kind during the early school years? How could you use the other subjects to help you?

# Discussion Eight

STUTTGART, AUGUST 29, 1919

Speech Exercise:

> In the vast unmeasured world-wide spaces,
> In the endless stream of time,
> In the depths of human soul-life,
> In the world's great revelations:
> Seek the unfolding of life's great mystery.

RUDOLF STEINER: The first four sentences have a ring of expectation, and the last line is a complete fulfillment of the first four. Now let's return to the other speech exercise:

> Proxy prized
> bather broomstick
> polka pushing
> beady basket
> prudent pertness
> bearskin bristled

RUDOLF STEINER: You can learn a great deal from this. And now we will repeat the sentence:

> Dart may these boats through darkening gloaming

RUDOLF STEINER: Also there is a similar exercise I would like to point out that has more feeling in it. It consists of four lines, which I will dictate to you later. The touch of feeling should be expressed more in the first line:

> Lulling leader limply
> liplessly laughing
> loppety lumpety
> lackety lout

RUDOLF STEINER: You must imagine that you have a green frog in front of you, and it is looking at you with lips apart, with its mouth wide open, and you speak to the frog in the words of the last three lines. In the first line, however, you tell it to lisp the lovely lyrics "Liebliche Lieder lallen." This line must be spoken with humorous feeling; you really expect this of the frog.

And now I will read you a piece of prose, one of Lessing's fables.[1]

## The Oak

One stormy night the raging north wind pitted its strength against a magnificent oak, which now lay on the ground. A number of low bushes lay shattered beneath it. A fox, whose lair was not far away, saw it next morning. "What a tree!" he cried, "I never would have thought it had been so big!"

RUDOLF STEINER: What is the moral of this fable?

---

1. Gotthold Ephraim Lessing (1729–1781), German dramatist, poet, critic, editor, and translator.

*Someone suggested: That it is not until someone is dead that we see
how great that person was. Another suggested: That, until the great
are overthrown, the small do not recognize what they were.*

Rudolf Steiner: But why then choose the fox, who is so cunning?

*Because the cunning of the fox cannot compare with the magnifi-
cence of the tree.*

RUDOLF STEINER: In which sentence would you find the
moral of the fable in relation to the cunning of the fox? "I
never would have thought it was so big!" The point is, he had
never even looked up; he had run round the bottom of the
trunk, which was the only part of the tree he had noticed, and
here the tree had only taken up a small space. Despite cunning, the fox had only seen what is visible around the foot of
the tree.

Please notice that fables—which by their very nature are
enacted in their own special world—can be read realistically,
but poems never.

Now the problem I placed before you yesterday brings us
something of tremendous importance, because now we must
consider what measures to take when we notice that one group
of children is less capable than another in one or another subject or lesson. I will ask you to choose from any part of the
period between six and fourteen, and to think especially of, let's
say, a group of children who cannot learn to read and write
properly, or those who cannot learn natural history or arithmetic, or geometry or singing. Consider what course you will
pursue in the class, or in your general treatment of the children, both now and later on, so that you can correct such
shortcomings as much as possible.

*Several teachers contributed detailed suggestions.*

RUDOLF STEINER: The examples you mention might arise partially from general incompetence. On the other hand, it could also be a question of a particular lack of talent. You could have children who are perhaps extraordinarily good at reading and writing, but as soon as they come to arithmetic they do not demonstrate any gift at all for it. Then there are those who are not so bad at arithmetic, but the moment you begin to call on their power of judgment, such as in natural science, their powers are at an end. Then again there are children who have no desire to learn history. It is important to notice these specific difficulties.

Perhaps you can find a remedy in this way: When you notice that a child, right from the beginning, has little talent for reading and writing, you would do well, anyway, to get in touch with the parents and ask them immediately to keep the child off eggs, puddings, and pastry as much as possible. The rest of the diet can remain more or less as it was. When the parents agree to try to provide the child with a really good wholesome diet, however—omitting the items of food mentioned above—they might even cut down on the meat for awhile and give the child plenty of vegetables and nourishing salads. You will then notice that, through a diet like this, the child will make considerable gains in ability. You must take advantage of this improvement, and keep the child very busy when the diet is first changed.

But if you notice that a mere change of diet doesn't help much, then, after you have talked it over with the parents, try for a short while, perhaps a week, to keep the child entirely without food for the whole morning, or at least the first part of the morning when the child should be learning to read and write—to allow learning on an empty stomach—or maybe give the child the minimum of food. (You should not continue too long with this method; you must alternate it with normal eating.) You must make good use of this time, however, when the capacities will most certainly be revealed, and the child will show greater ability and be more receptive to what you are teaching. If you repeat a cure of this kind several times over the year, you will see that the powers of a fairly young child undergo a change. This applies to the first years of school life. I ask you to consider this very seriously.

Generally speaking, you should be very aware that the foolish ways many parents feed their young children contributes greatly to the lessening of their faculties, especially with phlegmatic and sanguine children. Perpetually overfeeding children—and this is somewhat different at the present time,[2] but you should know these things—stuffing them with eggs, puddings, and starchy foods is one of the things that makes children unwilling to learn and incapable of doing so during the early years of their school life.

*A teacher asked about cocoa.*

RUDOLF STEINER: Why should children drink cocoa at all? It is not the least bit necessary except to regulate digestion. Things like this are needed sometimes for this purpose, and cocoa is better than other remedies for children whose digestion works too quickly, but it should not be included otherwise in children's diet. These days children are given many things that are unsuitable for them.

You can experience some very strange things in regard to this. When I was a teacher in the eighties, there was a young child in the house; I did not actually teach him, since I had only the older children; he was a little cousin. He was really a nice lovable child with bright ideas. He could have become a

---

2. Due to the food shortages in Germany in 1919.

gifted pupil. I saw him a good deal and could observe for myself how witty and gifted the child was. One day at table this little fellow—although he was scarcely two years old—had two little dumplings, and when someone said to him, "Look Hans, now you already have two dumplings," he was clever enough to answer, "And the third will follow in a minute." That's what the little tyke said!

Then another thing: he was very fond of calling people bad names. This did not seem very important to me in a child of that age—he would soon grow out of it. He had gotten into the habit of being particularly abusive to me. One day as I was coming in the door (he was a little older by this time) he stood there and blocked the way. He couldn't think of any name bad enough for me, so he said: "Here come two donkeys!" That was really very smart of him, wasn't it?

But the boy was pale; he had very little appetite and was rather thin. So, on the advice of an otherwise excellent doctor, this child was given a small glass of red wine with every meal. I was not responsible for him and had no influence in this extraordinary way of treating a child's health, but I was very concerned about it. Then in his thirty-second or thirty-third year I saw this individual again; he was a terribly nervous man. When he was not present I enquired what he had been like as a schoolboy. This restless man, although only in his thirties, had become very nervous, and demonstrated the lamentable results of that little glass of red wine given to him with his meals as a boy. He was a gifted child, for a child who says "Here come two donkeys" really shows talent.

*Frau Steiner interjected, "What an impudent boy!"*

RUDOLF STEINER: We needn't bother with impudence, but how does this really come about? It's amazing. He can find no word bad enough, and so he makes use of number to help him. That shows extraordinary talent. But he became a poor scholar and never wanted to learn properly. Thus, because of this method of treatment—giving him wine as a young child—he was completely ruined by the time he was seven years old.

This is what I want to impress upon you at the beginning of our talk today—that, in relation to a child's gifts and abilities, it is not the least unimportant to consider how to regulate the diet. I would especially ask you, however, to see that the child's digestion does not suffer. So when it strikes you that there is something wrong with a child's capacities, you must in some tactful way find out from the parents whether or not the child's digestion is working properly, and if not you should try to put it in order.

*Someone spoke about the children who are not good at arithmetic.*

Rudolf Steiner: When you discover a special weakness in arithmetic, it would be good to do this: generally, the other children will have two gymnastics lessons during the week, or one eurythmy lesson and one gymnastics lesson; you can take a group of the children who are not good at arithmetic, and allow them an extra hour or half-hour of eurythmy or gymnastics. This doesn't have to mean a lot of extra work for you: you can take them with others who are doing the same kind of exercises, but you must try to improve these children's capacities through gymnastics and eurythmy. First give them rod exercises. Say to them, "Hold the rod in your hand, first in front counting 1, 2, 3, and then behind 1, 2, 3, 4." Each time the child must change the position of the rod, moving it from front to back. A great effort will be made in some way to get the rod around behind at the count of 3. Then add walking: say, 3 steps forward, 5 steps back; 3 steps forward, 4 steps back; 5

steps forward, 3 steps back, and so on. In gymnastics, and also perhaps in eurythmy, try to combine numbers with the children's movements, so they are required to count while moving. You will find this effective. I have frequently done this with pupils.

But now tell me, why does it have an effect? From what you have already learned, you should be able to form some ideas on this subject.

*A teacher commented: Eurythmy movements must be a great help in teaching geometry.*

RUDOLF STEINER: But I did not mean geometry. What I said applied to arithmetic, because at the root of arithmetic is consciously willed movement, the sense of movement. When you activate the sense of movement in this way, you quicken a child's arithmetical powers. You bring something up out of the subconscious that, in such a child, is unwilling to be brought up. Generally speaking, when a child is bad both at arithmetic and geometry, this should be remedied by movement exercises. You can do a great deal for a child's progress in geometry with varied and inventive eurythmy exercises, and also through rod exercises.

*Comment: Where difficulties exist in pronunciation, the connection between speech and music should be considered.*

RUDOLF STEINER: Most cases of poor pronunciation are due to defective hearing.

*Comment: Sanguine students do not follow geography lessons very well because their ideas are vague. I recommend taking small portions of a map as subjects for drawing.*

RUDOLF STEINER: When you make your geography lessons truly graphic, when you describe the countries clearly and show the distribution of vegetation, and describe the products of the earth in the different countries, making your lessons thoroughly alive in this way, you are not likely to find your students dull in this subject. And when you further enliven the geography lessons by first describing a country, then drawing it—allowing the children, to draw it on the board and sketch in the rivers, mountains, distribution of vegetation, forest, and meadow land, and then read travel books with your pupils—when you do all this you find that you usually have very few dull scholars; and what's more, you can use your geography lessons to arouse the enthusiasm of your pupils and to stir up new capacities within them. If you can make geography itself interesting you will indeed notice that other capacities are aroused also in your pupils.

*Comment: I have been thinking about this problem in relation to the first three grades. I would be strict with lazy children and try to awaken their ambition. In certain cases children must be told that they might have to go through the year's work a second time. Emulation and ambition must be aroused.*

RUDOLF STEINER: I wouldn't recommend you to give much credit to ambition, which cannot generally be aroused in children. In the earliest school years you can make good use of the methods you suggest, but without overemphasizing ambition, because you would then later have to help the child to get rid of it again. But you must primarily consider food and diet, and I need to say this again and again.

Perhaps the friends who speak next will consider the fact that there are many children who in later life have no power of perceiving or remembering natural objects properly. A teacher may despair over some pupils who can never remember which among a number of minerals is a malachite or a hornblende, or even an emerald—who really have no idea of how to comprehend natural objects and recognize them again. The same is true also in relation to plants and animals. Please keep this in mind also.

*Comment: I have noticed that with the youngest children you often find some who are backward in arithmetic. I like best to illustrate everything to them with the fingers, or pieces of paper, balls, or buttons. One can also divide the class without the children knowing anything about it; they are divided into two groups, the gifted ones and the weaker ones. We then take the weaker ones alone so that the gifted children are not kept back.*

RUDOLF STEINER: In that case, Newton, Helmholtz, and Julius Robert Mayer would have been among the backward ones!

*That doesn't matter.*

RUDOLF STEINER: You are right. It doesn't matter at all. Even Schiller would have been among the weaker ones. And according to Robert Hamerling's teaching certificate, he passed well in practically everything except German composition; his marks for that subject were below average![3]

We have heard how eurythmy can help, and now Miss F. will tell us how she thinks eurythmy can be developed for the obstinate children, for they too must learn eurythmy.

*Miss F.: I think melancholic children would probably take little interest in rhythmic exercises and rod exercises, beating time or indeed any exercise that must be done freely, simply, and naturally.*

---

3. Robert Hamerling (1830–1889) was a distinguished German poet and a personal friend of Rudolf Steiner.

*They like to be occupied with their own inner nature, and they easily tire because of their physical constitution. Perhaps, when the others are doing rod exercises these children could accompany them with singing, or reciting poems in rhythm. In this way they will be drawn into the rhythm without physical exertion.*

*But it is also possible that melancholic children may dislike these exercises, because they have the tendency to avoid entering whole-heartedly into anything, and always withhold a part of their being. It would be good, therefore, to have them accompany the tone gestures with jumps, because the whole child must then come into play, and at the same time such gestures are objective.*

*The teacher must never feel that the child cannot do this, but instead become conscious that eurythmy, in its entirety, is already in the child. Such assurance on the part of the teacher would also be communicated to the child.*

RUDOLF STEINER: These suggestions are all very good. With regard to the children who resist doing eurythmy, there is still another way to get them to take pleasure in it. Besides allowing them to watch eurythmy frequently, try to take photographs of various eurythmy positions. These must be simplified so that the child will get visual images of the human being doing eurythmy forms. Pictures of this kind will make an impression on the children and kindle their abilities in eurythmy. That was why I asked Miss W. to take pictures of this kind (I don't mean mere reproductions of eurythmy positions, but transformed into simple patterns of movement that have an artistic effect). These could be combined to show children the beauty of line. You would then discover an exceptionally interesting psychological fact—that children could perceive the beauty of line that they produced themselves in eurythmy, without becoming vain and coy. Although children are likely to become vain if their attention is drawn to what they have themselves done, this is not the case in eurythmy. In eurythmy, therefore, you can also cultivate a perception of line that can be used to enhance the feeling of self without awakening vanity and coquettishness.

*Someone spoke of how he would explain the electric generator to children. He would try to emphasize in every possible way what would show the fundamental phenomenon most clearly.*

RUDOLF STEINER: That is a very important principle, and it is also applicable to other subjects. It is a good principle for teaching, but to a certain extent it applies to all children in the physics lessons. It has no direct connection with the question of dealing with backward pupils. In physics the backward ones, especially the girls, are certain to put up a certain amount of opposition, even when you show them a process of this kind.

*Question: Since food plays such a very important role, would Dr. Steiner tell us more about the effect of different foods on the body.*

RUDOLF STEINER: I have already spoken of this, and you can also find many references in my lectures. It would perhaps lead us too far afield today to go into all the details of this subject, but most of all one should avoid giving children such things as tea and coffee.

The effect of tea on our thoughts is that they do not want to cohere; they flee from one another. For this reason tea is very good for diplomats, whose job in life is just to keep talking, with no desire to develop one thought logically out of another. You should avoid sending children's thoughts into flight by allowing them to indulge in tea.

Neither is coffee good for children, because it disposes them to become too pedantic. Coffee is a well-known expedient for journalists, because with its help they can squeeze one thought out of another, as it were. This would not be the right thing for children, because their thoughts should arise naturally, one from another. Coffee and tea are among the things to be avoided.

The green parts of a plant and also milk may be considered especially important food for children, and they should have white meat only, as far as possible.

*Comment: When a child has difficulty in understanding, the teacher should offer a great deal of individual help, and should also inquire about how the child does in other subjects; but if too much time is spent with the duller children, the difficulty would arise that the others are left unoccupied.*

RUDOLF STEINER: Please do not overestimate what the other children lose because of your work with the less gifted ones. As a rule, not much is lost provided that, while you present a subject properly for the duller children, you also succeed in getting the brighter ones to pay attention to it also. There is really then no serious loss for the more talented children. When you have a right feeling for the way in which a subject should be introduced for the weaker ones, then in one way or another the others will profit by it.

*Comment: Whenever there is lack of interest, I would always have recourse to artistic impressions. I know of one child who cannot remember the forms of different minerals—in fact he finds it diffi-cult to form a mental image of any type of formation. Such chil-dren cannot remember melodies either.*

RUDOLF STEINER: You have discovered the particular difficulty found in children who have no perception of forms and no power of retaining them in memory. But you must distinguish between forms related to the organic world and those connected with minerals, which in fact run parallel to the forms of melodies. The important thing is that here we touch on a very, very radical defect, a great defect in the development of the child, and you must consider seriously how this defect can be fundamentally healed. There is an excellent way of helping these children to remember organic forms in nature—the forms of plants and animals; draw caricatures for them that emphasize the characteristics of a particular animal or plant. These drawings must not be ugly or in bad taste, but artistic and striking; now have the children try to remember these caricatures so that, in this roundabout way through caricature, they begin to find it easier to remember the actual forms. You could, for example, draw a mouse for them like this. Give it teeth and whiskers too if you like!

Then there is also another way of possibly helping children to grasp forms: have them understand from inside what they cannot grasp from outside. Let's suppose, for example, that a child cannot understand a parallelepiped from outside.[4] The child cannot remember this form. You say to the child: imagine you are a tiny little elf, and that you could stand inside of this form as if it were a room. You allow the child to grasp from inside what cannot be understood from outside. This the child can do. But you must repeat this again and again.

---

4. A *parallelepiped* is a solid with six sides, all of which are parallelograms.

With forms of this kind, which also appear in minerals, this is relatively easy to do, but it is not as easy when it comes to perceiving color or any other quality of the mineral. In that case you can help the child to understand merely by letting the imagination see that a small thing is very large indeed. Have the child repeatedly try to picture some little yellow crystal as a gigantic crystallized form.

When you are dealing with the element of time, however—in music, for example—it is not such an easy matter. Let us for the moment suppose that you have not yet made any progress in improving the children's grasp of *spatial* forms. Now, however, if you want to use caricature in *musical* form, you will only succeed when you introduce an arithmetical process, making the intervals infinitely larger and drawing out each sound for a very long time; thus by greatly increasing the time between each sound, you can produce the melody on a much larger scale, which will have an astonishing effect on the children. In this way you will achieve something, but otherwise you will not be able to effect much improvement.

Questions for tomorrow:

1. How can I treat the higher plants from a natural-scientific viewpoint in the same spirit shown yesterday for the animals, for cuttlefish, mouse, and human beings?[5]
2. How can I introduce mushrooms, mosses, and lichens into these lessons?

These two questions can perhaps be answered together. It is a case of applying the same methods for the plants as those I spoke of yesterday. It is not a question of object lessons, but of the proper teaching after the ninth year, when natural history is introduced into the curriculum.

---

5. See *Practical Advice to Teachers,* lecture 7.

# Discussion Nine

Speech exercise.

Deprive me not of what, when I give it to you freely,
pleases you.

Rudolf Steiner: This sentence is constructed chiefly to show the
break in the sense, so that it runs as follows: First the phrase
"*Deprive me not of what*," and then the phrase "*pleases you*," but
the latter is interrupted by the other phrase, "*when I give it to
you freely*." This must be expressed by the way you say it. You
must notice that the emphasis you dropped on the word
"*what*" you pick up again at "*pleases you*."

> Rateless ration
> roosted roomily
> reason wretched
> ruined Roland
> royalty roster

> Name neat Norman on nimble moody mules

> Piffling fifer
> prefacing feather
> phlegma fluting
> fairground piercing

Weekly verse from *The Calendar of the Soul*:

> I feel a strange power bearing fruit,
> Gaining strength, bestowing me on myself,
> I sense the seed ripening
> And presentiment weaving, full of Light,
> Within me on my selfhood's power.[1]

RUDOLF STEINER: Now we arrive at the difficult task before us today. Yesterday I asked you to consider how you would prepare the lessons in order to teach the children about the lower and higher plants, making use of some sort of illustration or example. I have shown you how this can be done in the case of animals—with a cuttlefish, a mouse, a horse, and a person—and your botany lessons must be prepared in the same spirit. But let me first say that the correct procedure is to study the animal world *before* coming to terms with the natural conditions of the plants. In the efforts necessary to characterize the form of your botany lessons—finding whatever examples you can from one plant or another—you will become clear why the animal period must come first.

Perhaps it would be a good idea if we first ask who has already given botany lessons. That person could speak first and the others can follow.

*Comment: The plant has something like an instinctive longing for the Sun. The blossoms turn toward the Sun even before it has risen. Point out the difference between the life of desire in animals and people, and the pure effort of the plant to turn toward the Sun. Then give the children a clear idea of how the plant exists between*

---

1. Verse for August 25–31 (twenty-first week); see Rudolf Steiner, *The Calendar of the Soul*, Anthroposophic Press, Hudson, NY, 1988.

*Sun and Earth. At every opportunity mention the relation of the plant to its surroundings, especially the contrast between plants and human beings, and plants and animals. Talk about the out-breathing and in-breathing of the plant. Allow the children to experience how "bad" air is the very thing used by the plant, through the power of the Sun, to build up again what later serves as food for people. When speaking of human dependence on food you can point to the importance of a good harvest, and so on. With regard to the process of growth it should be made clear that each plant, even the leaf, grows only at the base and not at the tip. The actual process of growth is always concealed.*

RUDOLF STEINER: What does it actually mean that a leaf only grows at the base? This is also true of our fingernails, and if you take other parts of the human being, the skin, the surfaces of the hands, and the deeper layers, the same thing applies. What actually constitutes growth?

*Comment: Growth occurs when dead matter is "pushed out" of what is living.*

RUDOLF STEINER: Yes, that's right. All growth is life being pushed out from inside, and the dying and gradual peeling off of the outside. That is why nothing can ever grow on the outside. There must always be a pushing of substance from within outward, and then a scaling off from the surface. That is the universal law of growth—that is, the connection between growth and matter.

*Comment: Actually the leaf dies when it exposes itself to the Sun; it sacrifices itself, as it were, and what happens in the leaf also happens at a higher level in the flower. It dies when it is fertilized. Its only life is what remains hidden within, continuing to develop.*

*With the lower plants one should point out that there are plants—mushrooms, for example—that are similar to the seeds of the higher plants, and other lower plants resemble more particularly the leaves of the higher plants.*

RUDOLF STEINER: Much of what you have said is good, but it would also be good in the course of your description to acquaint your students with the different parts of a single plant, because you will continually have to speak about the parts of the plant—leaf, blossom, and so on. It would therefore be good for the pupil to get to know certain parts of a plant, always following the principle that you have rightly chosen—that is, the study of the plant in relation to Sun and Earth. That will bring some life to your study of the plants; from there you should build the bridge to human beings. You have not yet succeeded in making this connection, because everything you said was more or less utilitarian—how plants are useful to people, for example—and other external comparisons.

There is something else that must be worked out before these lessons can be of real value to the children; after you have made clear the connection between animal and human being, you must also try to show the connection between plant and human being. Most of the children are in their eleventh year when we begin this subject, and at this point the time is ripe to consider what the children have already learned—or rather, we must keep in mind that the children have already learned things in a certain way, which they must now put to good use. Then too you must not forget to give the children the kind of image of the plant's actual form that they can understand.

*Comment: The germinating process should be demonstrated to the children—for example, in the bean. First the bean as a seed and then an embryo in its different stages. We could show the children how the plant changes through the various seasons of the year.*

RUDOLF STEINER: This should not really be given to your students until they are fifteen or sixteen years old. If you did take it earlier you would see for yourself that the children who are still in the lower grades cannot yet fully understand the germinating process. It would be premature to develop this germinating process with younger children—your example of the bean and so on. That is foreign to the child's inner nature.

*I only meant to point out to the children the similarity between the young plant and the young animal, and the differences as well. The animal is cared for by its mother, and the plant comes into the world alone. My idea was to treat the subject in a way that would appeal more to the feelings.*

RUDOLF STEINER: Even so, this kind of presentation is not suitable for children; you would find that they could not understand it.

*Question: Can one compare the different parts of the plant with a human being? The root with the head, for example?*

RUDOLF STEINER: As Mr. T. correctly described, you must give plants their place in nature as a whole—Sun, Earth, and so on—and always remember to speak of them in relation to the universe. Then when you give the proper form to your lesson you will find that the children meet what you present with a certain understanding.

*Someone described how plants and human beings can be compared—a tree with a person, for example: human trunk = tree trunk; arms and fingers = branches and twigs; head = root. When a person eats, the food goes from above downward, whereas in a tree the nourishment goes from below upward. There is also a difference: whereas people and animals can move around freely and feel pleasure and pain, plants cannot do this. Each type of plant corresponds to some human characteristic, but only externally. An oak is proud, while lichens and mosses are modest and retiring.*

RUDOLF STEINER: There is much in what you say, but no one has tried to give the children an understanding of the plant itself in its various forms. What would it be like if, for example, you perhaps ask, "Haven't you ever been for a walk during the summer and seen flowers growing in the fields, and parts of them fly away when you blow on them? They have little 'fans' that fly away. And you have probably seen these same flowers a little earlier, when summer was not quite so near; then you saw only the yellow leaf shapes at the top of the stem; and even earlier, in the spring, there were only green leaves with sharp jagged edges. But remember, what we see at these three different times is all exactly the same plant! Except that, to begin with, it is mainly a green leaf; later on it is mainly blossom; and still later it is primarily fruit. Those are only the fruits that fly around. And the whole is a dandelion! First it has leaves—green ones; then it presents its blossoms, and after that, it gets its fruit.

"How does all this happen? How does it happen that this dandelion, which you all know, shows itself at one time with nothing but green leaves, another time with flowers, and later with tiny fruits?

"This is how it comes about. When the green leaves grow out of the earth it is not yet the hot part of the year. Warmth does not yet have as much effect. But what is around the green leaves? You know what it is. It is something you only notice when the wind passes by, but it is always there, around you: the air. You know about that because we have already talked about it. It is mainly the air that makes the green leaves sprout, and then, when the air has more warmth in it, when it is hotter, the leaves no longer remain as leaves; the leaves at the top of the stem turn into flowers. But the warmth does not just go to the plant; it also goes down into the earth and then back again. I'm sure that at one time or another you have seen a little piece of tin lying on the ground, and have noticed that the tin first receives the warmth from the Sun and then radiates it out again. That is really what every object does. And so it is also with warmth. When it is streaming downward, before the soil itself has become very warm, it forms the blossom. And when the warmth radiates back again from the earth up to the plant, it is working more to form the fruit. And so the fruit must wait until the autumn."

This is how you should introduce the organs of the plant, at the same time relating these organs to the conditions of air and heat. You can now go further, and try to elaborate the thoughts that were touched on when we began today, showing the plants in relation to the outer elements. In this way you can also connect morphology, the aspect of the plant's form, with the external world. Try this.

*Someone spoke about plant-teaching.*

RUDOLF STEINER: Some of the thoughts you have expressed are excellent, but your primary goal must be to give the children a comprehensive picture of the plant world as a *whole*: first the lower plants, then those in between, and finally the higher plants. Cut out all the scientific facts and give them a pictorial survey, because this can be tremendously significant in your teaching, and such a method can very well be worked out concerning the plant world.

*Several teachers spoke at length on this subject. One of them remarked that "the root serves to feed the plant."*

RUDOLF STEINER: You should avoid the term *serves*. It's not that the root "serves" the plant, but that the root is related to the watery life of earth, with the life of juices. It is however not what the plant draws out of the ground that makes up its main nourishment, but rather the carbon from the air.

Children cannot have a direct perception of a metamorphosis theory, but they can understand the relationship between water and root, air and leaves, warmth and blossoms.

It is not good to speak about the plants' fertilization process too soon—at any rate, not at the age when you begin to teach botany—because children do not yet have a real understanding of the fertilization process. You can describe it, but you'll find that they do not understand it inwardly.

Related to this is the fact that fertilization in plants does not play as prominent a part as generally assumed in our modern-day, abstract, scientific age. You should read Goethe's beautiful essays, written in the 1820s, where he speaks of pollination and so on. There he defends the theory of metamorphosis over the actual process of fertilization, and strongly protests the way people consider it so terribly important to describe a meadow as a perpetual, continuous "bridal bed!" Goethe strongly disapproved of giving such a prominent place to this process in plants. Metamorphosis was far more important to him than the matter of fertilization. In our present age it is impossible to share Goethe's belief that fertilization is of secondary importance, and that the plant grows primarily on its own through metamorphosis; even though, according to modern advanced knowledge, you must accept the importance of the fertilization process, it still remains true, however, that we are doing the wrong thing when we give it the prominence that is customary today. We must allow it to retire more into the background, and in its place we must talk about the relationship between the plant and the surrounding world. It is far more important to describe the way air, heat, light, and water work on the plant, than to dwell on the abstract fertilization process, which is so prominent today. I want to really emphasize this; and because this is a very serious matter and particularly important, I would like you to cross this Rubicon, to delve further into the matter, so that you find the proper method of dealing with plants and the right way to teach children about them.

Please note that it is easy enough to ask what similarities there are between animal and humankind; you will discover this from many and diverse aspects. But when you look for similarities between *plants* and humankind, this external method of comparison quickly falls apart. But let's ask ourselves: Are we perhaps on the wrong path in looking for relationships of this kind at all?

Mr. R. came closest to where we should begin, but he only touched on it, and he did not work it out any further.

We can now begin with something you yourselves know, but you cannot teach this to a young child. Before we meet again, however, perhaps you can think about how to clothe, in language suited to children, things you know very well yourselves in a more theoretical way.

We cannot just take human beings as we see them in life and compare them with the plant; nevertheless there are certain resemblances. Yesterday I tried to draw the human trunk as a

kind of imperfect sphere.[2] The other part that belongs to it—
which you would get if you completed the sphere—indeed has
a certain likeness to the plant when you consider the mutual
relationship between plants and human beings. You could even
go further and say that if you were to "stuff" a person (forgive
the comparison—you will find the right way of changing it for
children) especially in relation to the middle senses, the sense of
warmth, the sense of sight, the sense of taste, the sense of smell,
then you would get all kinds of plant forms.[3] If you simply
"stuffed" some soft substance into the human being, it would
assume plant forms. The plant world, in a certain sense, is a
kind of "negative" of the human being; it is the complement.

In other words, when you fall asleep everything related to
your soul passes out of your body; these soul elements (the I
and the actual soul) reenter your body when you awaken. You
cannot very well compare the plant world with the body that
remains lying in your bed; but you can truthfully compare it
with the soul itself, which passes in and out. And when you
walk through fields or meadows and see plants in all the bright-
ness and radiance of their blossoms, you can certainly ask yourselves: What temperament is revealed here? It is a fiery
temperament! The exuberant forces that come to meet you
from flowers can be compared to qualities of soul. Or perhaps
you walk through the woods and see mushrooms or fungi and
ask: What temperament is revealed here? Why are they not
growing in the sunlight? These are the phlegmatics, these
mushrooms and fungi.

So you see, when you begin to consider the human element of
soul, you find relationships with the plant world everywhere,
and you must try to work out and develop these things further.

---

2. See *Practical Advice to Teachers,* lecture 7.
3. See *The Foundations of Human Experience,* lecture 8.

You could compare the animal world to the human body, but the plant world can be compared more to the soul, to the part of a human being that enters and "fills out" a person when awaking in the morning. If we could "cast" these soul forms we would have the forms of the plants before us. Moreover, if you could succeed in preserving a person like a mummy, leaving spaces empty by removing all the paths of the blood vessels and nerves, and pouring into these spaces some very soft substance, then you would get all kinds of forms from these hollow shapes in the human body.

The plant world is related to human beings as I have just shown, and you must try to make it clear to the children that the roots are more closely related to human thoughts, and the flowers more related to feelings—even to passions and emotions.

And so it happens that the most perfect plants—the higher, flowering plants—have the least animal nature within them; the mushrooms and the lowest types of plant are most closely akin to animals, and it is particularly these plants that can be compared least to the human soul.

You can now develop this idea of beginning with the soul element and looking for the characteristics of the plants, and you can extend it to all the varieties of the plant world. You can characterize the plants by saying that some develop more of the fruit nature—the mushrooms, for example—and others more of the leaf nature, such as ferns and the lower plants, and the palms, too, with their gigantic leaves. These organs, however, are developed differently. A cactus is a cactus because of the rampant growth of its leaves; its blossom and fruit are merely interspersed among the luxuriant leaves.

Try now to translate the thought I indicated to you into language suited for children. Exert your fantasy so that by next time you can give us a vivid description of the plant world all over the Earth, showing it as something that shoots forth into herb and flower, like the soul of the Earth, the visible soul, the soul made manifest.

And show how the different regions of Earth—the warm zone, the temperate zone, and the cold zone—each has its prevailing vegetation, just as in a human being each of the various spheres of the senses within the soul make a contribution. Try to make it clear to yourself how one whole sphere of vegetation can be compared with the world of sound that a person receives into the soul, another with the world of light, yet another with the world of smell, and so on.

Then try to bring some fruitful thoughts about how to distinguish between annuals and perennials, or between the flora of western, central, and eastern European countries. Another fruitful thought that you could come to is about how the whole Earth is actually asleep in summer and awake in winter.

You see, when you work in this way you awaken in the child a real feeling for intimacy of soul and for the truth of the spirit. Later, when the children are grown, they will much more easily understand how senseless it is to believe that human existence, as far as the soul is concerned, ceases every evening and begins again each morning. Thus they will see, when you have shown them, that the relationship between the human body and soul can be compared to the interrelationship between the human world and the plant world. How then does the Earth affect the plant? Just as the human body works, so when you come to the plant world you have to compare the human body with the Earth—and with something else, as you will discover for yourselves.

I only wanted to give you certain suggestions so that you, yourselves, using all your best powers of invention, can discover even more before next time. You will then see that you greatly benefit the children when you do not give them external comparisons, but those belonging to the inner life.

# Discussion Ten

Speech Exercises:

Children chiding
Chaffinch chirping
Choking chimneys
Cheerfully chattering

Children chiding and fetching
Chaffinch chirping switching
Choking chimneys hitching
Cheerfully chattering twitching

Beach children chiding and fetching
Reach chaffinch chirping switching
Birches choking chimneys hitching
Perches cheerfully chattering twitching

RUDOLF STEINER: The "ch" should be sounded in a thoroughly active way, like a gymnastic exercise.[1]

The following is a piece in which you have to pay attention both to the form and the content.

---

1. The original German exercise (which appears in the appendix) uses the "pf" sound; the "ch" sound has been substituted in the English version.

From *"Galgenlieder"* by Christian Morgenstern:

### The Does' Prayer

The does, as the hour grows late,
Med-it-ate;
Med-it-nine;
Med-i-ten;
Med-eleven;
Med-twelve;
Mednight!
The does, as the hour grows late,
Meditate,
They fold their little toesies,
the doesies.[2]

RUDOLF STEINER: Now we will continue our talk about the plant world.

*Various contributions were offered by those present.*

RUDOLF STEINER: Later there will be students in the school who will study the plant kingdom on a more scientific basis, in which case they would learn to distinguish mosses, lichens, algae, monocotyledons, dicotyledons, and so on. All children, who in their youth learn to know plants according to scientific principles, should *first* learn about them as we have described— that is, by comparing them with soul qualities. Later they can study the plant system more scientifically. It makes a difference whether we try first to describe the plants and then later study them scientifically, or vice versa. You can do much harm by

---

2. Max Knight, trans., University of California Press, Berkeley, 1964.

teaching scientific botany first, instead of first presenting ideas that relate to the feeling life, as I have tried to show you. In the latter case the children can tackle the study of scientific botanical systems with a truly human understanding.

The plant realm is the soul world of the Earth made visible. The carnation is a flirt. The sunflower an old peasant. The sunflower's shining face is like a jolly old country rustic. Plants with very big leaves would express, in terms of soul life, lack of success in a job, taking a long time with everything, clumsiness, and especially an inability to finish anything; we think that someone has finished, but the person is still at it. Look for the soul element in the plant forms!

When summer approaches, or even earlier, sleep spreads over the Earth; this sleep becomes heavier and heavier, but it only spreads out spatially, and in autumn passes away again. The plants are no longer there, and sleep no longer spreads over the Earth. The feelings, passions, and emotions of people pass with them into sleep, but once they are there, those feelings have the appearance of plants. What we have invisible within the soul, our hidden qualities—flirtatiousness, for example—become visible in plants. We don't see this in a person who is awake, but it can be observed clairvoyantly in people who are sleeping. Flirtation, for example, looks like a carnation. A flirt continually produces carnations from the nose! A tedious, boring person produces gigantic leaves from the whole body, if you could see them.

When we express the thought that the Earth sleeps, we must go further: the plant world grows in the summer. Earth sleeps in the summer and is awake during winter. The plant world is the Earth's soul. Human soul life ceases during sleep, but when the Earth goes to sleep its soul life actually begins. But the human soul does not express itself in a sleeping person. How are we going to get over this difficulty with children?

*One of the teachers suggested that plants could be considered the Earth's dreams.*

RUDOLF STEINER: But plants during high summer are not the Earth's dreams, because the Earth is in a deep sleep in the summer. It is only how the plant world *appears* during spring and autumn that you can call dreams. Only when the flowers are first beginning to sprout—when the March violet, for example, is still green, before flowers appear, and again when leaves are falling—that the plant world can be compared to dreams. With this in mind, try to make the transition to a real understanding of the plant.

For example, you can begin by saying, "Look at this buttercup," or any plant we can dig out of the soil, showing the root below, the stalk, leaves, blossoms, and then the stamens and pistil, from which the fruit will develop. Let the child look at a plant like this. Then show a tree and say, "Imagine this tree next to the plant. What can you tell me about the tree? Yes, it also has roots below of course; but instead of a stalk, it has a trunk. Then it spreads its branches, and it's as if the real plants grew on these branches, because many leaves and flowers can be found there; it's as if little plants were growing on the branches above. So, we could actually look at a meadow this way: We see yellow buttercups growing all over the meadow; it is covered with individual plants with their roots in the Earth, and they cover the whole meadow. But when we look at the tree, it's as if someone had taken the meadow, lifted it up, and rounded it into an arch; only then do we find many flowers growing very high all over it. The trunk is a bit of the Earth itself. So we may say that the tree is the same as the meadow where the flowers grow.

"Now we go from the tree to the dandelion or daisy. Here there is a root-like form in the soil, and from it grows something like a stalk and leaves, but at the top there is a little basket of flowers, tiny little blossoms close together. It's as though the dandelion made a little basket up there with nothing in it but little flowers, perfect flowers that can be found in the dandelion-head. So we have the tree, the little 'basket-bloomers,' and the ordinary plant, a plant with a stalk. In the tree it's as though the plants were only high up on the branches; in the compound flowers the blossom is at the top of the plant, except that these are not petals, but countless fully-developed flowers.

"Now imagine that the plant kept everything down in the Earth; suppose it wanted to develop roots, but that it was unsuccessful—or perhaps leaves, but could not do this either; imagine that the only thing to unfold above ground were what one usually finds in the blossom; you would then have a mushroom. At least, if the roots down below fail and only leaves come up, you would then have ferns. So you find all kinds of different forms, but they are all plants."

Show the children the buttercup, how it spreads its little roots, how it has its five yellow-fringed petals, then show them the tree, where the "plant" only grows on it, then the composite flowers, the mushroom, and the fern; do not do this in a very scientific way, but so that the children get to know the form in general.

Then you can say, "Why do you think the mushroom remained a mushroom, and why did the tree become a tree? Let's compare the mushroom with the tree. What is the difference between them? Take the tree. Isn't it as though the Earth had pushed itself out with all its might—as though the inner being of the tree had forced its way up into the outside world in order to develop its blossoms and fruits away from the Earth? But in the mushroom the Earth has kept within itself what usually grows up out of it, and only the uppermost parts of the plant appear in the form of mushrooms. In the mushroom the 'tree' is below the soil and only exists as forces. In the mushroom itself we find something similar to the tree's outermost part. When lots and lots of mushrooms are spread over the Earth, it is as though you had a tree growing down below them, inside the Earth. And when we look at a tree it is as though the Earth had forced itself up, turning itself inside out, as it were, bringing its inner self into the outer world."

Now you are coming nearer to the reality: "When you see mushrooms growing you know that the Earth is holding something within itself that, in the case of a growing tree, it pushes up outside itself. So in producing mushrooms the Earth keeps the force of the growing tree within itself. But when the Earth lets the trees grow it turns the growing-force of the tree outward."

Now here you have something not found within the Earth during summer, because it rises out of the Earth then and when winter comes it goes down into the Earth again. "During summer the Earth, through the force of the tree, sends its own force up into the blossoms, causing them to unfold, and in winter it draws this force back again into itself. Now let us think of this force, which during the summer circles up in the trees—a force so small and delicate in the violet but so powerful in the tree. Where can it be found in winter? It is under the surface of the Earth. What happens during the depth of winter to all these plants—the trees, the composite flowers, and all the others? They unfold right under the Earth's surface; they are there within the Earth and develop the Earth's soul life. This was known to the people of ancient times, and that was why they placed Christmas—the time when we look for soul life—not in the summer, but during winter.

"Just as a person's soul life passes out of the body when falling asleep, and again turns inward when a person wakens, so it is also for the Earth. During summer while asleep it sends its sap-bearing force out, and during winter takes it back again when it awakens—that is, it gathers all its various forces into itself. Just think, children, our Earth feels and experiences everything that happens within it; what you see all the summer long in flowers and leaves, the abundance of growth and blossom, in the daisies, the roses, or the carnations—this all dwells under the Earth during winter, and there it has feelings like you have, and can be angry or happy like you."

In this way you gradually form a view of life lived under the Earth during winter. That is the truth. And it is good to tell the children these things. This is something that even materialists could not argue with or consider an extravagant flight of fancy. But now you can continue from this and consider the whole plant. The children are led away from a subjective attitude toward plants, and they are shown what drives the sap over the Earth during summer heat and draws it back again into itself in winter; they come to see the ebb and flow in plant life.

In this way you find the Earth's real soul life mirrored in plants. Beneath the Earth ferns, mosses, and fungi unfold all that they fail to develop as growing plants, but this all remains etheric substance and does not become physical. When this etheric plant appears above the Earth's surface, the external forces work on it and transform it into the rudiments of leaves we find in fungi, mosses, and ferns. But under a patch of moss or mushrooms there is something like a gigantic tree, and if the Earth cannot absorb it, cannot keep it within itself, then it pushes up into the outer world.

The tree is a little piece of the Earth itself. But what remains underground in mushrooms and ferns is now raised out of the Earth, so that if the tree were slowly pushed down into the Earth everything would be different, and if it were to be thus submerged then ferns, mosses, and mushrooms would appear; for the tree it would be a kind of winter. But the tree withdraws from this experience of winter. It is the nature of a tree to avoid

the experience of winter to some extent, but if I could take
hold of a fern or a mushroom by the head and draw it further
and further out of the Earth so that the etheric element in it
reached the air, then I would draw out a whole tree, and what
would otherwise become a mushroom would now turn into a
tree. Annual plants are midway between these two. A composite flower is merely another form of what happens in a tree. If I
could press a composite flower down into the Earth it would
bear only single blossoms. A composite flower could almost be
called a tree that has shot up too quickly.

And so we can also find a wish, a desire, living in the Earth.
The Earth feels compelled to let this wish sink into sleep. The
Earth puts it to sleep in summer, and then the wish rises as a
plant. It is not visible above the Earth until it appears as a
waterlily. Down below it lives as a wish in the Earth, and then
up above it becomes a plant.

The plant world is the Earth's soul world made visible, and
this is why we can compare it with human beings. But you
should not merely make comparisons; you must also teach the
children about the actual forms of the plants. Starting with a
general comparison you can then lead to the single plant species.

Light sleep can be compared with ordinary plants, a kind of
waking during sleep with mushrooms (where there are very
many mushrooms, the Earth is awake during the summer), and
you can compare really sound deep sleep with the trees.

From this you see that the Earth does not sleep as people do,
but in one part it is more asleep and in another more awake;
here more asleep, there more awake. People, in their eyes and
other sense organs, also have sleeping, waking, and, dreaming
side by side, all at the same time.

Now here is your task for tomorrow. Please make out a table;
on the left place a list of the human soul characteristics, from
thoughts down through all the emotions of the soul—feelings

of pleasure and displeasure, actively violent emotions, anger, grief, and so on, right down to the will; certain specific plant forms can be compared with the human soul realm. On the right you can then fill in the corresponding plant species, so that in the table you have the thought plants above, the will plants below, and all the others in between.

Rudolf Steiner then gave a graphic explanation of the Pythagorean theorem and referred to an article by Dr. Ernst Müller in Ostwald's magazine for natural philosophy, *Annalen der Naturphilosophie*, entitled "Some Observations on a Theory of Knowledge underlying the Pythagorean theorem."

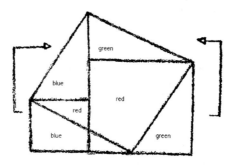

In the drawing, the red parts of the two smaller squares already lie within the square on the hypotenuse. By moving the blue and the green triangles in the direction of the arrows, the remaining parts of the two smaller squares will cover those parts of the square on the hypotenuse still uncovered.

You should cut out the whole thing in cardboard and then you can see it clearly.[3]

---

3. The Pythagorean theorem states that the square of the hypotenuse of a right triangle is equal to the sum of the squares of the other two sides. For another brief discussion of the Pythagorean theorem in teaching see Rudolf Steiner, *The Kingdom of Childhood: Introductory Talks on Waldorf Education*, Anthroposophic Press, Hudson, NY, 1995, pp. 85–90.

# Discussion Eleven

STUTTGART, SEPTEMBER 2, 1919

RUDOLF STEINER: In the speech exercises that we will take now, the principal purpose is to make the speech organs more flexible.

> Curtsey Betsy jets cleric
> lastly light sceptic

One should acquire the habit of letting the tongue say it on its own, so to speak.

> Tu-whit twinkle 'twas
> twice twigged tweaker
> to twenty twangy twirlings
> the zinnia crisper
> zither zooming shambles
> this smartened smacking
> smuggler sneezing
> snoring snatching.

Both these exercises are really perfect only when they are said from memory.

From "We Found a Path" (by Christian Morgenstern):

> Those who don't know the goal
> can't find the way,
> they will trot the same circle
> all their lives long,
> and return in the end
> whence they began,
> their piece of mind
> more disturbed than before.

RUDOLF STEINER: Now we will proceed to the task that we have been gnawing at for so long.

*Someone presented a list of the human soul moods and the soul moods of plants that could be said to correspond to them.*

RUDOLF STEINER: All these things that have been presented are reminiscent of when phrenology was in vogue, when people classified human soul qualities according to their fantasies, and then searched the head for all kinds of bumps that were then associated with these qualities. But things are not like that, although the human head can certainly be said to express human soul nature. It is true that if a person has a very prominent forehead, it may indicate a philosopher. If a person has a very receding forehead and is at the same time talented, such a person may become an artist. You cannot say that the artist is located in a particular part of the head, but through your feelings you can differentiate between one or another form. You should consider the soul in this way. The more intellectual element drives into the forehead, and the more artistic element allows the forehead to recede. The same thing is also true in the study of plants. I mean your research should not be so external, but rather you should enter more deeply into the inner nature of plants and describe conditions as they actually are.

*Some remarks were added.*

RUDOLF STEINER: When you confine yourself too much to the senses, your viewpoint will not be quite correct. The senses come into consideration insofar as each sense contributes to the inner life of human beings, whatever can be perceived by a particular sense. For example, we owe several soul experiences to the sense of sight. We owe different soul experiences to other senses. Thus we can retrace our soul experiences to these various senses. In this way the senses are associated with our soul nature. But we should not assert unconditionally that plants express the senses of the Earth, because that is not true.

*Someone cited samples from the writings of Emil Schlegel, a homeopathic doctor from Tübingen.*

RUDOLF STEINER: Schlegel's comparisons are also too external. He returns to what can be found in the mystics—Jacob Boehme and others—to the so-called "signatures." Mystics in the Middle Ages were aware of certain relationships to the soul world that led them into deeper aspects of medicine. You find, for example, that a definite group of plants is associated with a quality of soul; mushrooms and fungi are associated with the quality that enables a person to reflect, to ponder something, the kind of inner life that lies so deeply in the soul that it does not demand much of the outer world for its experience, but "pumps," as it were, everything out of itself. You will also find that this soul quality, most characteristic of mushrooms, is very intimately associated with illnesses of a headache nature; in this way you discover the connection between mushrooms and illnesses that cause headaches. Please note that you cannot make such comparisons when teaching about animals.

There are, as yet, no proper classifications of plants, but by means of these relationships between human soul qualities and groups of plants you must try to bring some kind of classification into the life of plants. We will now attempt to classify the plant kingdom.

You must first distinguish what are properly seen as the different parts of the plant—that is, root, stem (which may develop into a trunk), leaves, blossoms, and fruits. All the plants in the world can be divided into groups or families. In one family the root is more developed; the rest of the plant is stunted. In another the leaves are more developed, and in others the blossoms; indeed, these last are almost entirely blossom. Such things must be considered in relation to each other. Thus we can classify plants by seeing which system of organs predominates, root, trunk, leaves, and so on, since this is one way that plants vary. Now, when you recognize that everything with the nature of a blossom belongs to a certain soul quality, you must also assign other organic parts of the plant to other soul qualities. Thus, whether you associate single parts of the plant with qualities of soul or think of the whole plant kingdom together in this sense, it is the same thing. The whole plant kingdom is really a single plant.

Now what are the actual facts about the sleeping and waking of the Earth? At the present time [September] the Earth is asleep for us, but it is awake on the opposite side of the Earth. The Earth carries sleep from one side to the other. The plant world, of course, takes part in this change, and in this way you get another classification according to the spatial distribution of sleeping and waking on the earth—that is, according to summer and winter. Our vegetation is not the same as that on the opposite side of the Earth.

For plant life, everything is related with the leaves, for every part of a plant is a transformed leaf.

*Someone compared groups of plants with temperaments.*

RUDOLF STEINER: No, you are on the wrong track when you relate the plant world directly to the temperaments.

We might say to the children, "Look children, you were not always as big as you are now.[1] You have learned to do a great many things that you couldn't do before. When your life began you were small and awkward, and you couldn't take care of yourselves. When you were very small you couldn't even talk. You could not walk either. There were many things you could not do that you can do now. Let's all think back and remember the qualities you had when you were very young children. Can you remember what you were like then and what kinds of things you did? Can you remember this?" Continue to ask until they all see what you mean and say "No." "So none of you know anything about what you did when you were toddlers?

"Yes, dear children, and isn't there something else that happens in your lives that you can't remember, and things that you do that you can't remember afterward?" The children think it over. Perhaps someone among them will find the answer, otherwise you must help them with it. One of them might answer, "While I was asleep." "Yes, the very same thing happens when you are very young that happens when you go to bed and sleep. You are 'asleep' when you are a tiny baby, and you are asleep when you are in bed.

"Now we will go out into nature and look for something there that is asleep just like you were when you were very

---

1. According to the Waldorf curriculum, the children are around eleven years old when they are taught about the plant kingdom.

young. Naturally you could not think of this yourselves, but there are those who know, and they can tell you that all the fungi and mushrooms that you find in the woods are fast asleep, just as you were when you were babies. Fungi and mushrooms are the sleeping souls of childhood.

"Then came the time when you learned to walk and to speak. You know from watching your little brothers and sisters that little children first have to learn to speak and walk, or you can say walk and then speak. That was something new for you, and you could not do that when you began your life; you learned something fresh, and you could do many more things after you learned to walk and speak.

"Now we will go out into nature again and search for something that can do more than mushrooms and fungi. These are the algae," and I now show the children some examples of algae, "and the mosses," and I show them some mosses. "There is something in algae and mosses that can do much more than what is in the fungi."

Then I show the children a fern and say, "Look, the fern can do even more than the mosses. The fern can do so much that you have to say it looks as if it already had leaves. There is something of the nature of a leaf.

"Now you do not remember what you did when you learned to speak and walk. You were still half asleep then. But if you watch your brothers and sisters or other little children you know that, when they grow a little older, they do not sleep as long as when they were first born. Then came the time when your mind woke up, and you can return to that time as your earliest memory. Just think! That time in your mind compares with the ferns. But ever since then you can remember more and more of what happened in your mind. Now let's get a clear picture of how you came to say 'I.' That was about the time to which your memory is able to return.

But the I came gradually. At first you always said 'Jack wants...' when you meant yourself."

Now have a child speak about a memory from childhood. Then you say to the child, "You see, when you were little it was really as though everything in your mind was asleep; it was really night then, but now your mind is awake. It is much more awake now, otherwise you would be no wiser than you used to be. But you are still partly asleep; not everything in you is awake yet; much is still sleeping. Only a part of you has awakened. What went on in your mind when you were four or five years old was something like the plants I am going to show you now."

We should now show the children some plants from the family of the gymnospernms—that is, conifers, which are more perfectly formed than the ferns—and then you will say to the children, "A little later in your life, when you were six or seven years old, you were able to go to school, and all the joys that school brought blossomed in your heart." When you show a plant from the family of the ferns, the gymnosperms, you go on to explain, "You see there are still no flowers. That was how your mind was before you came to school.

"Then, when you came to school, something entered your mind that could be compared to a flowering plant. But you had only learned a little when you were eight or nine years old. Now you are very smart; you are already eleven years old and have learned a great many things.

"Now look; here is a plant that has leaves with simple parallel veins

and here is another with more complicated leaves with a network of veins. When you look at the blossoms that belong to the simple leaves, they are not the same as those on the plants with the other kind of leaf, where the blossoms and everything else are more complicated than in those with the simpler leaves."

Now you show the children, for example, an autumn crocus, a *monocotyledon*; in these plants everything is simple, and you can compare them to children between seven and nine. Then you can continue by showing the children plants with simple blossoms, ones that do not yet have real petals. You can then say, "You have plants here in which the green sepals and the colored petals are indistinguishable, in which the little leaves under the blossom cannot be distinguished from those above. This is you! This is what you are like now.

"But soon you will be even older, and when you are twelve, thirteen, or fourteen you will be able to compare yourselves with plants that have calyx and corolla; your mind will grow so much that you'll be able to distinguish between the green leaves we call the calyx and the colored leaves called petals. But first you must reach that stage!" And so you can divide the plants into those with a simple perianth—compared to the eleven-year-old children—and plants with a double perianth—those of thirteen to fourteen years.[2] "So children, this is another stage you have to reach."

Now you can show the children two or three examples of mosses, ferns, gymnosperms, *monocotyledons*, and *dicotyledons*, and it would be a fine thing at this point to awaken their memory of earlier years. Have one of them speak of something remembered about little four-year-old Billy, and then show your ferns; have another child recall a memory of seven-year-old Fred, and then show the corresponding plant for that age; and

---

2. The *perianth* is the envelope of a flower, particularly one in which the calyx and corolla are combined so that they are indistinguishable from one another; these include such flowers as tulips, orchids, and so on. The perianth is *single* when it has one verticil, and *double* when it has both calyx and corolla.

yet another one could tell a story about eleven-year-old Ernie, and here you must show the other kind of plant. You must awaken the faculty of recalling the various qualities of a growing child and then carry over to the plant world these thoughts about the whole development of the growing soul. Make use of what I said yesterday about a tree, and in this way you will get a parallel between soul qualities and the corresponding plants.

There is an underlying principle here. You will not find parallels accidentally according to whatever plants you happen to pick. There is principle and form in this method, which is necessary. You can cover the whole plant kingdom in this way, with the exception of what happens in the plant when the blossom produces fruit. You point out to the child that the higher plants produce fruits from their blossoms. "This, dear children, can only be compared to what happens in your own soul life after you leave school." Everything in the growth of the plant, up to the blossom, can be compared only with what happens in the child until puberty. The process of fertilization must be omitted for children. You cannot include it.

Then I continue, "You see, dear children, when you were very small you really only had something like a sleeping soul within you." In some way remind the children, "Now try to remember, what was your main pleasure when you were a little child? You have forgotten now because, in a way, you were really asleep at that time, but you can see it in little Anne or Mary, in your little baby sister. What is her greatest joy? Certainly her milk bottle! A tiny child's greatest joy is the milk bottle. And then came the time when your brothers and sisters were a little older, and the bottle was no longer their only joy, but instead they loved to be allowed to play. Now remember, first I showed you fungi, algae, mosses; almost everything they have, they get from the soil. We must go into the woods if we want to get to know them. They grow where it is damp and shady, they do not venture out into the sunlight. That's what you were like before you 'ventured out' to play; you were content with sucking milk from a bottle. In the rest of the plant world you find leaves and flowers that develop when the plants no longer have only what they get from the soil and from the shady woods, but instead come out into the sun, to the air and light. These are the qualities of soul that thrive in light and air." In this way you show the child the difference between what lives under the Earth's surface on the one hand (as mushrooms and roots do, which need the watery element, soil, and shade), and on the other hand, what needs air and light (as blossoms and leaves do). "That is why plants that bear flowers and leaves (because they love air and light) are the so-called higher plants, just as you, when you are five or six years old, have reached a higher stage than when you were a baby."

By directing the children's thoughts more and more—at one time toward qualities of mind and soul that develop in childhood, and then toward the plants—you will be able to classify them all, based on this comparison. You can put it this way:

Pleasures of infancy (babies):  Mushrooms and Fungi

Pleasures of early childhood (the awakening life of feeling, both sorrows and joys): Algae, Mosses

Experiences at the awakening of consciousness of self: Ferns

Experiences of fifth and sixth year, up to school age: Gymnosperms, Conifers

First school experiences, seventh, eighth, ninth, tenth and eleventh year: Parallel-veined plants, Monocotyledons;  Plants with simple perianth

Experiences of the eleven-year-old: Simple dicotyledons

School experiences from twelfth to fifteenth year:   Net-veined plants, Dicotyledons; Plants  with green calyx and colored petals

"You are not smart enough yet for these last experiences (the plants with a green calyx and colored blossoms), and you won't know anything about them until you are thirteen or fourteen years old.

"Just think; how lovely! One day you will have such rich thoughts and feelings, you will be like the rose with colored petals and green sepals. This will all come later, and you can look forward to it with great pleasure. It is lovely to be able to rejoice over what is coming in the future." The important thing is that you arouse within children's hearts a joyful anticipation of what the future will bring them.

Thus, all the successive soul qualities before puberty can be compared with the plant kingdom. After that the comparison goes no further because at this point the children develop the astral body, which plants do not possess. But when the plant forces itself into fertilization beyond its nature, it can be compared with soul qualities of the sixteenth to seventeenth year. There is no need to call attention to the process of fertilization, but you should speak of the process of growth, because that agrees with reality. The children would not understand the process of fertilization, but they would understand the process of growth, because it can be compared with the process of growth in the mind and soul. Just as a child's soul is different at various ages, so also the plants are different because they progress from the mushroom to the buttercup, which is usually included among the most highly developed plants, the *Ranunculuses*. It is indeed true that, when the golden buttercups appear during spring in lush meadows, we are reminded of the soul life and soul mood of fourteen-and fifteen-year-old boys and girls.

If at some time a botanist should go to work along these lines in a thoroughly systematic way, a plant system would be found that corresponds to fact, but you can actually show the children the whole external plant world as a picture of a developing

child's soul. Much can be done in this way. You should not differentiate in the individualized way practised by the old phre-
nologists, but you should have one clear viewpoint that can be
carried right through your teaching. Then you will find that it is
not quite correct to merely take everything with a root nature
and relate it to thought. Spirit in the head is still asleep in a
child. Thus, thinking in general should not be related to what
has root nature, but a child's way of thinking, which is still
asleep. In the mushroom, therefore, as well as in the child, you
get a picture of childlike thinking, still asleep, that points us
toward the root element in plants.

Rudolf Steiner then gave the following assignments:

1. To comprehensively work out the natural history of plants
as discussed up to this point;

2. The geographical treatment of the region of the lower
Rhine, from the Lahn onward, "in the way I showed you today
when speaking of lessons in geography": mountains, rivers,
towns, civilization, and economics.[3]

3. Do the same for the basin of the Mississippi.

4. What is the best way to teach the measurement of areas
and perimeters?

---

3. See *Practical Advice to Teachers*, lecture 11.

# Discussion Twelve

Speech Exercises:

> Curtsey cressets Betsy jets cleric
> lastly plotless light skeptic

RUDOLF STEINER: You will only get the words right when you can reel them off by heart. Be conscious of every syllable you speak!

> Narrow wren
> mirror royal
> gearing grizzled
> noting nippers
> fender coughing

*Some of the teachers, as requested, gave a comprehensive survey of the natural history of plants as discussed in yesterday's discussion.*

RUDOLF STEINER: Give as many examples as possible! Ideas about metamorphosis and germination cannot really be understood by children under the age of fourteen, and certainly not by children of nine to eleven. Related to this is something else of great importance that needs to be said. You must have followed the recent discussions from every side about so-called "sex education" for children. Every possible perspective, for and against, has been presented.

The subject essentially breaks down into three questions. First, we consider who should present such sex education. Those who think seriously about their great responsibility as teachers in the school soon realize the extraordinary difficulty of such an undertaking. I doubt if any of you would really welcome the job of providing sex education to young teenagers between twelve and fourteen. The second question concerns how this teaching should be given. This is not an easy question either. The third question is about its place in education. Where should you introduce it? In natural history lessons perhaps?

If teaching were based on true educational principles this task would fall very naturally into place. If in your teaching you explain the process of growth to the children in relation to light, air, water, earth, and so on, the children will absorb such ideas so that you can proceed gradually to the process of fertilization in plants, and then in animals and human beings. But you must look comprehensively at this matter and show how plants come into existence through light, water, earth, and so on; in short, for the complicated process of growth and fertilization you must prepare ideas that will provide children with a foundation in imaginative thinking. The fact that there has been so much chatter about sex education proves that there is something wrong with teaching methods of today; it should certainly be possible in the early school years to prepare for later sex education. For instance, by explaining the process of growth in connection with light, air, water, and so on, the teacher could foster the pure and chaste views necessary for sex education later on.

In map drawing you should color the mountains brown and rivers blue. Rivers should always be drawn as they flow, from source to mouth, never from mouth to source. Make one map for the soil and ground nature—coal, iron, gold, or silver, and draw another map for towns, industries, and so on. I ask you to note the importance of choosing some particular part of the world as a subject for your lessons, and then as you continue, you should refer back to this area again and again. The way that your subject is presented is also very important; try to live directly into your subject so that the children always get the feeling that you are describing something in which you are actually involved. When you describe an industry they should feel that you are working there, and the same is true when you describe a mine, and so on. Make it as lively as possible! The more life there is in your descriptions, the better the children will work with you.

*Someone calculated the measurement of areas, beginning with the square and proceeding to the rectangle, parallelogram, trapezium, and triangle.*

RUDOLF STEINER: It is difficult to explain to a child what an angle actually is. Can you make up a method for doing this? Perhaps you remember how difficult it was for you to be clear about it—aside from the fact that there may be some of you who do not yet know what an angle really is.

You can explain to the children what a larger or smaller angle is by drawing angles, first with longer arms and then with shorter arms. Now which angle is the larger? They are exactly the same size!

Then have two of the children walk from a certain point simultaneously, two times, and show them that the first time they walked they made a larger angle, and the second time a smaller one. When they walked making the smaller angle their paths were closer together, with the larger angle further apart. This can also be shown with an elbow movement.

It's good to arrive at a view of larger and smaller angles before beginning to measure angles in degrees.

*The transformation of a parallelogram into a square was spoken about, to show that the area, in both cases, is base multiplied by height.*

RUDOLF STEINER: Yes, it can be done like that. But if by tomorrow you would consider the whole subject on a somewhat different basis, perhaps you will find it beneficial to introduce the children to a clear concept of area as such first, and then the size of the area. The children know the shape of a square, and now you want to show it to them as a *surface* that could be larger or smaller.

Second, figure out for tomorrow how you would give the children arithmetical problems to solve without writing down any figures—in other words, what we could call mental arithmetic. You could, for example, give the children this problem to do: A messenger starts from a certain place and walks so many miles per hour; another messenger begins much later; the second messenger does not walk but rides a bicycle at a certain number of miles per hour. When did the cyclist pass the messenger on foot?

The object of these problems is to develop in children a certain presence of mind in comprehending a situation and evaluating it as a whole.

# Discussion Thirteen

Speech Exercises:

> Clip plop pluck cluck
> clinked clapper richly
> knotted trappings
> rosily tripled

RUDOLF STEINER: Memorize this *before* you practice it!

*An attempt was made to illustrate the concept of a surface area for nine-year-old children; have the children cut out squares to measure from larger squares and copy them.*

RUDOLF STEINER: It is certainly good to make it clear to children that, if the length of one side of a square is 3 feet, the area of the surface is 9 square feet, but this limits us to an area of thought where a whole is built from its parts, and this will not help children to gain a true concept of what a surface area really is. What I meant was: What is the right way to proceed, and at what age, in order to actually discover what a surface really is, and that it is obtained by multiplying length by breadth. How can you manage to awaken this concept of a surface in the child? This depends on when you begin teaching children about surface areas. It doesn't make sense to teach them about surface areas until after you teach them some algebra. The answer, therefore, is to wait for lessons on surface areas until after we deal with algebra.

Now comes another question: How do you make the transition from ordinary problems with figures to problems with letters—that is, algebra? I will give you a suggestion about how to begin, and then you can work it out for yourselves. Before you move on to algebra you must have already worked on *interest* with the children; *interest* is *principal* multiplied by *rate percent* multiplied by *time,* divided by 100.

Interest = Principal × Rate × Time

*or*   I = $\dfrac{PRT}{100}$

To arrive at this formula, begin with ordinary numbers, and children understand principal, rate percent, time, and so on, relatively easily. So you will try to make this process clear and assure yourself that most of the children have understood it; from there you should move on to the formula, and always make sure that you work according to rule.

*P = principal; R = rate; T = time; and I = interest.* What I gave you is a formula I view merely as a basic formula, and with this formula I have taken the first step in moving to algebra. When the children have this formula they merely need to substitute figures for the letters, and then they will always get the right answer.

Now if you have the following formula derived from the first:

P = $\dfrac{100\,I}{T\,R}$   you can see that you can change about the

3 letters *P, R, T,* however you wish, so that the following are also possibilities:

T = $\dfrac{100\,I}{P\,R}$              R = $\dfrac{100\,I}{P\,T}$

In this way we have taught the children how to work with *interest,* and now we can go on to algebra. You can simply say, "We have learned that a sum of 25 was equal to 8, then 7 and 5, and another 5: that is, $25 = 8 + 7 + 5 + 5$." The children will already have understood. Now after you have explained this, you can say, "Here, instead of 25 you could have a different number, and, instead of 8, 7, 5, 5 you could have other numbers; in fact, you could tell them that any number could be there. You could have *s*, for example, as a total, and then you could have $a + b + c + c$; but if c represents the first 5, then *c* must also represent the second 5. Just as I put *P* in place of *principal,* so in the same place I put the letter *c*.

After having shown in a concrete example the transition from number to letter you can now explain the concept of multiplication, and out of this concrete $g \times g$ you can develop $a \times a$, or from $a \times 2$ you can evolve $a \times b$, and so on. This then would be the way to progress from the numbers in arithmetic to algebra with its letters, and from algebra to the calculation of surface areas; $a \times a = a^2$.

Now here is your task for tomorrow. Try to find a truly enlightened way to present to children of ten and eleven the concept of interest and everything associated with it, as well as inverse calculations of rate, time, and principal; then from there demonstrate how to deal with discount—how to teach a child the discounting of bills and the cost of packing and conveyancing, and then continue on to bills of exchange and how to figure them out. That belongs to the twelfth and thirteenth year, and if it is taught at this time it will be retained for the rest of life; otherwise it is always forgotten again. It is possible to deal with it in a simpler form, but it should be done at this age. Anyone who can do this properly has mastered the fundamental method of all computation. Compound interest is not involved at this time. You should therefore go over algebra in an organic way until multiplication, and then continue on to surface area calculation.

Now let's proceed to the other questions from yesterday, because here it is important also that you should engender presence of mind in the children by assigning them problems.

*Someone proposed setting up a little stall with fruit, vegetables, potatoes, and so on, so that the children would have to buy and sell, pay for their purchases, and actually figure out everything for themselves.*

RUDOLF STEINER: This idea of buying and selling is very good for the second grade. Also, you should insist that those who have been assigned a problem should really work it out for themselves; you must not allow anyone else do it for them. Keep their interest awake and alive at every point!

*Mental arithmetic was discussed.*

RUDOLF STEINER related how Gauss[1] as a boy of six arrived at the following solution to a problem he had to do: all of the numbers from 1 to 100 had to be added together. Gauss thought about the problem and concluded it would be a simpler and easier to get a quick answer by taking the same numbers twice, arranging them in the first row in the usual order from left to right—1, 2, 3, 4, 5... up to 100, and beneath that a second row in the reverse order—100, 99, 98, 97, 96... and

---

1. Carl Friedrich Gauss (1777–1855), German mathematician and astronomer. He demonstrated that a circle can be divided into seventeen equal arcs through elementary geometry and developed a new technique for calculating the orbits of asteroids. He is also the originator of the *Gaussian error curve* in statistics and is considered the founder of the mathematical theory of electricity, from which derives the *gaussmeter.*

so on to 1; thus 100 was under the 1, 99 under the 2, 98 under the 3, and so on. Then each of these 2 numbers would in every case add up to the whole. This sum would then have to be taken 100 times, which makes 10,100; then, because you have added each of the numbers from 1 to 100 twice (once forward and once backward) this sum would then be halved, and the answer is 5,050. In this way Gauss, to the great astonishment of his teacher, solved the problem in his head.

*Along with some other things, two special problems were presented:*
*1. Calculation of time and distance for locomotives in which the circumferences of the wheels are of different sizes.*
*2. Exercises involving the filling and emptying of vessels with pipes of various sizes.*

RUDOLF STEINER: You can use your imagination in making up arithmetical problems, and you can engender presence of mind through problems that deal with movement. With yesterday's example you can progress to practical life by saying, "I sent an express messenger with a letter. Because of certain circumstances the letter was no longer valid. So I sent another messenger. How quickly must the second messenger travel to arrive before the letter had caused any harm? The children should be able to figure this out at least approximately, which is good for them.

*One of the teachers spoke of errors in calculation.*

RUDOLF STEINER: These kinds of errors in calculations are usual. It is very common to figure the errors into the whole. There is one such mistake made these days that will at sometime or another have to be corrected. When Copernicus formulated his "Copernican system" he proposed three laws. If all three were to be used to describe the Earth's course through space we would get a very different movement from what is now accepted by astronomers and taught in schools. This elliptic movement would only be possible if the third law were disregarded. When the astronomer uses the telescope, these things do not add up. Because of this, corrections are inserted into the calculations; through the use of Bessel's equations, corrections are introduced every year to account for what does not accord with reality.[2] In Bessel's corrections there is the third law of Copernicus.

Your method must never be simply to occupy the children with examples you figure out for them, but you should give them practical examples from real life; you must let everything lead into practical life. In this way you can always demonstrate how what you begin with is fructified by what follows and vice versa.

How would you resolve all these problems? (the flow of fluids slowly through small holes, quickly through large holes; rates of circular motion in machines with wheels of different sizes, and so on.)

The best way would be to proceed at this point to the explanation of what a clock is in its various forms—pendulum-clocks, watches, and so on.

These are your tasks for tomorrow:

1. Some historical subject related to the history of civilization to be worked out on the lines of the example.

2. The treatment of some subject taken from nature—sunrise and sunset, seasons of the year and so on—whatever may

---

2. Friedrich Wilhelm Bessel (1784–1846), German astronomer; he calculated the orbit of Halley's comet in 1804 and made the first "authenticated" calculation of a star's distance from Earth. He also calculated the elliptical nature of Earth's orbit.

suggest itself to you, something out of the great universe. The point is to show your method of teaching.

3. The principles of music for the first school year.

4. What form would you give to teaching the poetry of other languages? How would you give the children a feeling for what is poetic in other tongues?

5. How can you provide children with an idea of the ellipse, hyperbola, circle, and lemniscate; also the concept of geometrical locus? The children must be taught all this just before they leave our school at fourteen.

# Discussion Fourteen

*The principles were developed for teaching music to the first and second grades.*

RUDOLF STEINER: Children should be allowed to hear an instrument, to hear music objectively, apart from themselves. This is important. It should be a matter of principle that well before the ninth year the children should learn to play solo instruments, and the piano can be added later for those for whom it is considered advisable. What matters most is that we make a right beginning in this sphere.

*Further remark on the concept of interest, proceeding to algebra:*
*If $A$ = amount, $P$ = principal, $I$ = interest, $R$ = rate of interest, $T$ = time, then $A = P + I$.*

$$\text{Since } I = \frac{PRT}{100}$$
$$\text{then } A = P + \frac{PRT}{100}$$

RUDOLF STEINER: It would never be possible to describe capital in this way these days; this formula only has real value if $T$ equals a year or less, because in reality two cases are given: Either you remove the interest each year, in which case the same initial capital always remains, or else you leave the interest with the capital, in which case you need to figure according to compound interest. If you omit *T*—that is, if you figure it for only one year, then it is an actual thing; it is essential to present realities to the children. Do not fail to observe that the transition to algebra as we have spoken of it, is really carried out— first from addition to multiplication, and then from subtraction to division. This must be adhered to strictly.

RUDOLF STEINER explained the transition from arithmetic to algebra with the following example: First you write down a number of figures in which all the addenda are different:

$$20 = 7 + 5 + 6 + 2$$

Some of the addenda could also be equal:

$$25 = 5 + 5 + 9 + 6$$

Or all the addenda could be the same:

$$18 = 6 + 6 + 6$$

If you proceed, as described in our previous discussion, to replace numbers with letters, then you could have the equation:

$S_1 = a + a + a$; that is, three a's, or three times a = 3a.

then

$S_2 = a + a + a + a + a$; five times a = 5a;

then

$S_3 = a + a + a + a + a + a + a$; or seven times a = 7a

and so on. I can keep doing this; I could do it 9 times, 21 times, 25 times, I can do it *n* times:

$S_n = a + a + a \ldots\ldots$ n times = na

Thus, I get the factor by varying the number of the addenda, while the addendum itself is the other factor. In this way multiplication can easily be developed and understood from addition, and you thus make the transition from actual numbers to algebraic quantities:

$a \times a = a^2, a \times a \times a = a^3$.

In the same way you can derive division from subtraction. If we take $b$ away from a very large number $a$, we get the remainder $r$:

$r = a - b$

If we take $b$ away again, we get the remainder:

$r_2 = a - b - b = a - 2b$

If $b$ is taken away a third time we obtain:

$r_3 = a - b - b - b = a - 3b$ and so on.

We could continue until there is nothing left of number $a$: suppose this happens after subtracting $b$ $n$ times:

$r_n = a - b - b - b \ldots\ldots. n \text{ times} = -nb$

When there is nothing left—that is, when the last remainder is $0$, then:

$0 = a - nb$

So $a$ is now completely divided up, because nothing remains:

$a = nb$

I have taken $b$ away $n$ times, I have divided $a$ into nothing but $b$s, $\frac{a}{b} = n$, so the $a$ is completely used up. I have discovered that I can do this $n$ times, and in so doing I have gone from subtraction to division.

Thus we can say: multiplication is a special case of addition, and division is a special case of subtraction, except that you add to it or take away from it, not just once, but repeatedly, as the case may be.

*Negative and imaginary numbers were discussed.*

RUDOLF STEINER: A negative number is a *subtrahend* [the number subtracted] for which there is no *minuend* [the number from which it is subtracted]; it is a demand that something be done: there being nothing to do it with, thus it cannot be done. Eugen Dühring rejected imaginary numbers as nonsense and spoke of

Gauss's definition of "the imaginary" as completely stupid, unrealistic, farfetched nonsense.[1]

From addition, therefore, you develop multiplication, and from multiplication, rise to a higher power. And then from subtraction you develop division, and from division, find roots.

addition—subtraction
multiplication—division
raising to a higher power—finding roots

You should not proceed to raising to a higher power and finding roots until after you have begun algebra (between the eleventh and twelfth years), because, with roots, raising to a power of an algebraic equation of more than one term (*polynomial*) plays a role. In this connection you should also deal with figuring gross, net, taxes, and packing charges.

*A question about the use of formulas.*

RUDOLF STEINER: The question is whether you should avoid the habitual use of formulas, but go through the thought processes again and again (a good opportunity for practicing speech), or whether it might be even better to go ahead and use the formula itself. If you can succeed, tactfully, in making the formula fully understood, then it can be very useful to use it as a speech exercise—to a certain extent.

But from a certain age on, it is also good to make the formula into something *felt* by the children, make it into something that has inner life, so that, for example, when the $T$

---

1. Karl Eugen Dühring (1833–1921), German positivist philosopher and economist. Wrote *Kapital und Arbeit* (*Capital and Labor*), and *Logik und Wissenschaftstheorie* (*Logic and Epistemological Theory*).

increases in the formula $I = PRT/100$, it gives the children a feeling of the whole thing growing.

In effect, this is what I wanted to say at this point—that you should use the actual numbers for problems of this kind—for example, in interest and percentages—in order to make the transition to algebra, and in doing so, develop multiplication, division, raising powers, and roots. These are things that certainly must be done with the children.

Now I would like to ask a question: Do you consider it good to deal with raising to a higher power and finding roots before you have done algebra, or would you do it later?

*Comment about raising to a higher power first and finding roots after.*

RUDOLF STEINER: Your plan then would be (and should continue to be) to start with algebra as soon as possible after the eleventh or twelfth year, and only after that proceed to raising to a higher power and finding roots. After teaching the children algebra, you can show them in a very quick and simple way how to square, cube, raise to a higher power, and extract the root, whereas before they know algebra you would have to spend a terribly long time on it. You can teach easily and economically if you take algebra first.

*A historical survey for the older children (eleven to fourteen years) was presented concerning the founding and development of towns, referring to the existence of a "Germany" at the time of the invasion of the Magyars.*

RUDOLF STEINER: You must be very careful not to allow muddled concepts to arise unconsciously. At the time of Henry, the so-called "townbuilder," there was of course no "Germany."

You would have to express what you mean by saying "towns on the Rhine" or "towns on the Danube" in the districts that later became "German."[2]

Before the tenth century the Magyars are not involved at all, but there were invasions of Huns, Avars, and so on. But after the tenth century you can certainly speak of "Germany." When the children reach the higher grades (the seventh and eighth grades) I would try to give them a concept of chronology; if you just say ninth or tenth century, you do not give a sufficiently real picture. How then would you manage to awaken in the children a concrete view of time?

You could explain it to them like this: "if you are now of such and such an age, how old are your mother and father? Then, how old are your grandfather and grandmother?" And so you evoke a picture of the whole succession of generations, and you can make it clear to the children that a series of three generations makes up about 100 years, so that in 100 years there would be three generations. A century ago the great grandparents were children. But if you go back nine centuries, there have not been three generations, but 9 x 3 = 27 generations. You can say to the child: "Now imagine you are holding your father's hand, and he's holding your grandfather's hand, and he is, in turn, holding your great-grandfather's hand, and so on. If they were now all standing together side by side, which would be Henry I, which number in the row would have stood face to face with the Magyars around the year 926? It would be the twenty-seventh in the row." I would demonstrate this very clearly in a pictorial way. After giving the children this concrete image of how long ago it was, I would present a graphic description of the migrations of the Magyars. I would

---

2. This could as well apply to speaking of "America" in regard to events and places prior to the time of Columbus and the European settlers.

tell them about the Magyars' invasion of Europe at that time, how they broke in with such ferocity that everyone had to flee before them, even the little children in their cradles, who had to be carried up to the mountaintops, and how then the onrushing Magyars burned the villages and forests. Give them a vivid picture of this Magyar onset.

*It was then described how Henry, knowing he had been able to resist the Magyars in fortified Goslar, resolved to build fortified towns, and in this way it come about that numerous towns were founded.*

RUDOLF STEINER: Here again, could you not present this more in connection with the whole history of civilization? It is only a garbled historical legend to say that Henry founded these towns. All these tenth century towns were built on their original foundations—that is, the markets—before then. But what helped them to expand was the migration of the neighboring people into the towns in order to defend themselves more easily against the Magyars' assaults, and for this reason they fortified these places. The main reasons for building these towns were more economic in nature. Henry had very little part in all this.

I ask you to be truly graphic in your descriptions, to make everything really alive, so that the children get vivid pictures in their minds, and the whole course of events stands out clearly before them. You must stimulate their imagination and use methods such as those I mentioned when I showed you how to make time more real. Nothing is actually gained by knowing the year that something occurred—for example, the battle of Zama; but by using the imagination, by knowing that, if they held hands with all the generations back to Charles the Great, the time of their thirtieth ancestor, the children would get a truly graphic, concrete idea of time. This point of time then grows much closer to you—it really does—when you know that Charles the Great is there with your thirtieth ancestor.

*Question: Wouldn't it also be good when presenting historical descriptions to dwell on the difference in thought and feeling of the people of those times?*

RUDOLF STEINER: Yes. I have always pointed this out in my lectures and elsewhere. Most of all, when speaking of the great change that occurred around the fifteenth century, you should make it very clear that there was a great difference between the perception, feeling, and thought of people before and after this time. Lamprecht too (whom I do not however especially recommend) is careful to describe a completely different kind of thinking, perceiving, and feeling in people before this time.[3] The documents concerning this point have not yet been consulted at all.

In studying the books written on cultural history you must, above all, develop a certain perceptive faculty; with this you can properly assess all the different things related by historians, whether commonplace or of greater importance, and so gain a truer picture of human history.

Rudolf Steiner recommended for the teachers' library Buckle's *History of Civilization in England* and Lecky's *History of Rationalism in Europe.*

RUDOLF STEINER: From these books you can learn the proper methods of studying the history of human progress. With Lamprecht only his earlier work would be suitable, but even much of this is distorted and subjective. If you have not

---

3. Karl Gottfried Lamprecht (1856–1915), historian who developed the theory that history is social-psychological rather than political.

acquired this instinct for the real forces at work in history, you will be in danger of falling into the stupidity and amateurism of a "Wildenbruch" for example;[4] he imagined that the stories of emperors and kings and the family brawls between Louis the Pious and his sons were important events in human history.

Gustav Freytag's *Stories from Ancient German History* are very good;[5] but you must beware of being influenced too much by this rather smug type of history book (written for the unsophisticated). The time has come now when we must get out of a kind of thinking and feeling that belonged to the middle of the nineteenth century.

*Mention was made of Houston Stuart Chamberlain's* Foundations of the Nineteenth Century.[6]

RUDOLF STEINER: With regard to Chamberlain also you must try to develop the correct instinct. For one part of clever writing you get three parts of bad, unwholesome stuff. He has some very good things to say, but you must read it all yourselves and form your own judgements. The historical accounts of Buckle and Lecky are better.[7] Chamberlain is more one of these "gentlemen in a dinner jacket." He is rather a vain person and cannot be accepted as an authority, although many of his observations are correct. And the way he ended up was not particularly nice—I mean his lawsuit with the "Frankfurter Zeitung."

4. Ernst von Wildenbruch (1845–1909), German writer, author of *Spartacus.*
5. Gustav Freytag (1816–1895), German writer, promoter of German liberalism and the middle class. His books included a series of six historical novels.
6. Houston Stuart Chamberlain (1855–1927), British publicist, naturalized German citizen. Wrote on the superiority of the Western Aryan race.
7. Probably refers to Henry Thomas Buckle (1821–1862), English historian, who wrote the incomplete *History of Civilization in England.* William Edward Hartpole Lecky 1838–1903), Irish historian who wrote on modern European history.

*Kautsky's writings were mentioned.*[8]

RUDOLF STEINER: Well yes, but as a rule you must assume that the opposite of what he says is true! From modern socialists you can get good material in the way of facts, as long as you do not allow yourselves to be deceived by the theories that color all their descriptions. Mehring too presents us with rather a peculiar picture;[9] because at first, when he was himself a progressive Liberal, he inveighed against the Social Democrats in his book on Social Democracy; but later when he had gone over to the Social Democrats he said exactly the same things about the Liberals!

*An introduction was presented on the fundamental ideas in mathematical geography for twelve-year-old children, with observations on the sunrise and the ecliptic.*

RUDOLF STEINER: After taking the children out for observations, it would be very good to let them draw what they had observed; you would have to make sure there is a certain parallel between the drawing and what the children saw outside. It is advisable not to have them do too much line drawing. It is very important to teach these things, but if you include too much you will reach the point where the children can no longer understand what you are saying. You can relate it also to geography and geometry.

When you have developed the idea of the ecliptic and of the coordinates, that is about as far as you should go.

---

8. Karl Johann Kautsky (1854–1938), German Marxist theorist, journalist, and secretary to Friedrich Engels in London, he opposed Bolshevism and the Russian revolution.
9. Franz Mehring (1846–1919), German Socialist historian and journalist.

*Someone else developed the same theme—that is, sunrise and sun-set—for the younger children, and tried to explain the path of the Sun and planets in a diagrammatic drawing.*

RUDOLF STEINER: This viewpoint will gradually lose more and more of its meaning, because what has been said until now about these movements is not quite correct. In reality it is a case of a movement like this (lemniscatory screw-movement):

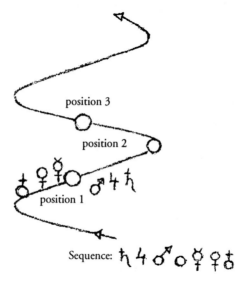

Here, for example, [in position 1] we have the Sun; here are Saturn, Jupiter, Mars, and here are Venus, Mercury, and Earth. Now they all move in the direction indicated [spiral line], moving ahead one behind the other, so that when the Sun has progressed to the second position we have Saturn, Jupiter, and Mars here, and we have Venus, Mercury, and Earth over there. Now the Sun continues to revolve and progresses to here [position 3]. This creates the illusion that Earth revolves round the Sun. The truth is that the Sun goes ahead, and the Earth creeps continually after it.

*The ancient Egyptian civilization was described.*

RUDOLF STEINER: It is most important to explain to the children that Egyptian art was based on a completely different method of representing nature. The ancient Egyptians lacked the power of seeing things in perspective. They painted the face from the side and the body from the front. You may certainly explain this to the children, especially the Egyptian concept of painting. Then you must point out how Egyptian drawing and painting was related to their view of natural history—how, for example, they portrayed men with animal heads and so on.

In ancient times the habit of comparing people with the animals was very common. You could then point out to the children what is present in seed form, as it were, within every human face, which children can still see to a certain extent.[10] The Egyptians still perceived this affinity of the human physiognomy with animals; they were still at this childlike stage of perception.

*Question: What should one really tell children about the building of the Egyptian pyramids?*

RUDOLF STEINER: It is of course extraordinarily important for children too that you should gradually try to present them with what is true rather than what is false. In reality the pyramids were places of initiation, and this is where you reach the point of giving the children an idea of the higher Egyptian education, which was initiation at the same time. You must tell them something about what happened within the pyramids. Religious services were conducted there, just as today they are conducted in churches, except that their services led to knowledge

---

10. See *The Foundations of Human Experience,* lecture 9.

of the universe. Ancient Egyptians learned through being shown, in solemn ritual, what comes about in the universe and in human evolution. Religious exercises and instruction were the same; it was really such that instruction and religious services were the very same thing.

*Someone described the work of the Egyptians on the pyramids and obelisks, and said that several millions of people must have been needed to transport the gigantic blocks of stone, to shape them, and to set them in place. We must ask ourselves how it was possible at all, with the technical means available at that time, to move these great heavy blocks of limestone and granite and to set them in place.*

RUDOLF STEINER: Yes, but you only give the children a true picture when you tell them: If people were to do this work with the physical strength of the present day, two and a half times as many people would be necessary. The fact is that the Egyptians had two and a half times the physical strength that people have today; this is true, at least, of those who worked on the pyramids and so on. There were also, of course, those who were not so strong.

*Question: Would it be good to include Egyptian mythology?*

RUDOLF STEINER: Unless you can present Egyptian mythology in its true form, it should be omitted. But in the Waldorf school, if you want to go into this subject at all, it would be a very good plan to introduce the children to the ideas of Egyptian mythology that are true, and are well known to you.[11]

---

11. See Rudolf Steiner, *Egyptian Myths and Mysteries*, Anthroposophic Press, Hudson, NY, 1990.

# Discussion Fifteen

Speech Exercises:

> Slinging slanging a swindler
> the wounding fooled a victor vexed
> The wounding fooled a swindler
> slinging slanging vexed
>
> March smarten ten
> clap rigging rockets
> Crackling plopping lynxes
> fling from forward forth
>
> Crackling plopping lynxes
> fling from forward forth
> March smarten ten
> clap rigging rockets

RUDOLF STEINER: With this exercise you should share the recitation, like a relay race, coming in quickly one after the other. One begins, points to another to carry on, and so on.

*Someone spoke about the ellipse, the hyperbola, the circle, the lemniscate, and the conception of geometrical loci. At the same time he mentioned how the lemniscate (Cassini curve) can take on the form III, in the diagram, where the one branch of the curve leaves space and enters space again as the other branch.*

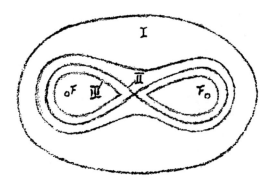

RUDOLF STEINER: This has an inner organic correlate. The two parts have the same relation to each other as the pineal gland to the heart. The one branch is situated in the head—the pineal gland, the other lies in the breast—the heart. Only the pineal gland is more weakly developed, the heart is stronger.

*Someone spoke on a historical theme—the migrations of various peoples.*

RUDOLF STEINER: The causes assigned to such migrations very often depend on the explanations of historical facts. As to the actual migrations—for example, the march of the Goths—at the root of the matter, you will find that the Romans had the money and the Germanic peoples had none, and at every frontier there was a tendency among the Germanic peoples to try to acquire Roman money one way or another. Because of this, they became mercenaries and the like. Whole legions of the Germanic peoples entered into Roman hire. The migration of the people was an economic matter. This was the only thing that made the spread of Christianity possible, but the migrations as such began, nevertheless, with the avarice of the Germanic peoples who wanted to acquire Roman money. The Romans of course were also impoverished by this. This was already the case as early as the march of the Cimbri. The Cimbri were told that the Romans had money, whereas they themselves were poor. This had a powerful effect on the Cimbri. "We want gold," they cried, "Roman gold!"

There are still various race strata—even Celtic traces. Today there are definite echoes of the Celtic language—for example, at the sources of the Danube, Brig and Breg, Brigach, and Brege, and wherever you find the suffix *ach* in the place names such as *Unterach, Dornach*, and so on. *Ach* comes from a word meaning a "small stream" (related to aqua), and points to a Celtic origin. "Ill," too, and other syllables remind us of the old Celtic language. The Germanic language subsequently overlaid the Celtic.

[Rudolf Steiner referred to the contrast between Arians and Athanasians.[1]]

There is something connected with the history of these migrations that is very important to explain to the children— that is, that it was very different for the migrating peoples to come into districts that were already fully developed agriculturally. In the case of the Germanic peoples, such as the Goths in Spain and Italy, they found that all the land was being cultivated already. The Goths and other ethnic groups arrived but soon disappeared. They became absorbed by the other nations who were there before them. The Franks, on the other hand, preferred to go to the West, and arrived in districts not yet fully

---

1. *Athanasian* refers to the doctrine of Saint Athanasius, or Athanasius the Great (c. 293–373), who was a Greek theologian and prelate in Egypt. Throughout his life he opposed Arianism and became known as the "Father of Orthodoxy." He was exiled three times by Roman emperors for his stand; he wrote *Four Orations against the Arians* but not the Athanasian Creed (written after the fifth century), which espouses his teachings on the Trinity. The Arian doctrine, on the other hand, has to do with Arius (c. 250–336), also a Greek ecclesiastic in Alexandria, who taught a Neoplatonic doctrine that God is alone and unknowable, the creator of every being, including the Christ. Emperor Constantine I formed the Council of Nicaea in 325 to declare Arianism a heresy.

claimed for agriculture, and they continued to exist as Franks. Nothing remained of the Goths who settled where the land was all already owned. The Franks were able to preserve their nationality because they had migrated into untilled areas. That is a very important historical law. You can refer to this law again later in relation to the configuration of North America. There, it is true that the Red Indians were almost exterminated, but it was also true, nevertheless, that people could migrate into uncultivated districts.

It is also important to explain the difference between such things as, for example, the France of Charles the Great and the state of a later time. If you are unaware of this difference, you cannot cross the Rubicon of the fifteenth century. The empire of Charles the Great was not yet a state. How was it for the Merovingians? Initially they were no more than large-scale landowners. The only thing that mattered to them was civil law. As time passed, this product of the old Germanic conditions of ownership became the Roman idea of "rights," whereby those who were merely administrators gradually acquired power. And so, by degrees, property went to the administrative authorities, the public officials, and the state arose only when these authorities became the ruling power later. The state, therefore, originated through the claims of the administration. The "count nobility" arose as the antithesis of "prince nobility." The word *Graf* (count) has the same origin as "graphologist" or "scribe." It is derived from *graphein*, to write. The "count" is the Roman scribe, the administrator, whereas the "prince nobility," originally the warrior nobility, is still associated with bravery, heroism, and similar qualities. The prince (*Fürst*) is "first," the foremost one. And so this transition from *Fürst* to *Graf* (prince to count) marked the rise of the concept of "state." This can of course be made very clear by using examples such as these.

*Someone described how he would introduce the spread of Christianity among the Germanic peoples.*

RUDOLF STEINER: Arian Christianity, expressed in practical life, is very similar to later Protestantism, except that it was less abstract and more concrete. During the first and second centuries the Mithras cult was very widespread among Roman soldiers on the Rhine and the Danube, especially among the officers. In what is now Alsace and elsewhere, Thor, Wotan, and Saxnot were worshipped as the three principal gods of the ancient Germanic people, and the old Germanic religious rites and ceremonies were used.[2]

We could describe many scenes that demonstrate how the little churches were built in Alsace and the Black Forest by the Roman clerics. "We want to do this or that for Odin" sang the men. The women sang, "Christ came for those who do *nothing* by themselves." This trick was actually used to spread Christianity—that by doing nothing one could achieve salvation.

*Eiche* (the oak), in the old Germanic cult-language, designates the priest of Donar. During the time of Boniface it was still considered very important that the formulas were still known. Boniface knew how to gain possession of some of these formulas; he knew the magic word, but the priest of Donar no longer knew it. Boniface, through his higher power, felled the priest of Donar—the "Donar-oak"—by means of his "axe," the magic word. The priest died of grief; he perished through the "fire from Heaven." These are images of imagination. Several generations later this was all transformed into the well-known picture.

---

2. This is a reference to Steiner's lectures on the history of the Middle Ages, given in the Workers' College in Berlin between October 18 and December 20, 1904 *Geschichte des Mittelalters bis zu den großen Erfindungen und Entdeckungen* (GA 51).

You must learn to "read" pictures of this kind, and thus through learning to teach, and through teaching to learn.

Boniface romanized Germanic Christianity. Charles the Great's biography was written by Eginhard, and Eginhard is a flatterer.

*Music teaching was spoken about.*

RUDOLF STEINER: Those who are less advanced in music should at least be present when you teach the more advanced students, even if they do not take part and merely listen. You can always separate them later as a last resort. There will be many other subjects in which the situation will be just as bad, in which it will be impossible for the more advanced students to work with those who are backward. This will not happen as often if we keep trying to find the right methods. But due to a variety of circumstances, such things are not obvious now. When you really teach according to our principles you will discover that the difficulties, usually unnoticed, will appear not only in music lessons, but in other subjects as well—for example, in drawing and painting. You will find it very difficult to help some of the children in artistic work, and also in the plastic arts, in modeling.

Here, too, you should try not to be too quick to separate the children, but try to wait until they can no longer work together.

*Someone spoke about teaching poetry in French and English [foreign language] lessons.*

RUDOLF STEINER: We must stay strictly with speaking a certain amount of English and French with the children right from the beginning—not according to old-fashioned methods, but so that they learn to appreciate both languages and get a feeling for the right expressions in each.

When a student in the second, third, or fourth grade breaks down over recitation, you must help in a kind and gentle way, so that the child trusts you and doesn't lose courage. The child's good will must also be aroused for such tasks.

The lyric-epic element in poetry is suitable for children between twelve and fifteen years of age, for example, ballads or outstanding passages from historical writings, good prose extracts, and selected scenes from plays.

Then in the fourth grade we begin Latin, and in the sixth grade Greek for those who want it, and in this way they can get a three-year course. If we could enlarge the school we would begin Latin and Greek together. We shall have to see how we can manage to relieve children who are learning Latin and Greek of some of their German. This can be done very easily, because much of the grammar can be dealt with in Latin and Greek, which would otherwise come into the German lessons. There can also be various other ways.

*C* was pronounced "*K*" in old Latin; and in medieval Latin, which was a spoken language, it was *C* as in "cease." The ancient Romans had many dialects in their empire. We can call *Cicero* "Sisero" because in the Middle Ages it was still pronounced like that. We can't speak of what is "right" in pronunciation because it is something quite conventional. The method of teaching classical languages can be similarly constructed; here, however, with the exception of what I referred to this morning,[3] it is usually possible to use the normal contemporary curricula, because they originated in the best educational periods of the Middle Ages, and they still contain much that has pedagogical value for teaching Latin and Greek.

3. See morning lecture pp. 189–190.

Today's curricula still copy from the old, which makes good sense.

You should avoid one thing, however: the use of the little doggerel verses composed for memorizing the rules of grammar. To the people of today they seem rather childish, and when they are translated into German they are just too clumsy. You must try to avoid these, but otherwise such methods are not at all bad.

Sculpting should begin before the ninth year. With sculpture too, you should work from the forms—spheres first, then other forms, and so on.

*Someone asked whether reports should be provided.*

RUDOLF STEINER: As long as children remain in the same school, what is the purpose of writing reports? Provide them when they leave school. Constant reports are not vitally important to education. Remarks about various individual subjects could be given freely and without any specific form.

Necessary communication with the parents is in some cases also a kind of grading, but that cannot be entirely avoided. It may also prove necessary, for example, for a pupil to stay in the same grade and repeat the year's work (something we should naturally handle somewhat differently than is usual); this may be necessary occasionally, but in our way of teaching it should be avoided whenever possible. Let's make it our practice to correct our students so that they are really *helped* by the correction.

In arithmetic, for example, if we do not stress what the child *cannot* do, but instead work with the student so that in the end the child *can* do it—following the opposite of the principle used until now—then "being unable" to do something will not play the large role it now does. Thus in our whole teaching, the passion for passing judgment that teachers acquire by marking grades for the children every day in a notebook should be transformed into an effort to help the children over and over, every moment. Do away with all your grades and placements. If there is something that the student cannot do, the teachers should give themselves the bad mark as well as the pupil, because they have not yet succeeded in teaching the student how to do it.

Reports have a place, as I have said, as communication with the parents and to meet the demand of the outside world; in this sense we must follow the usual custom. I don't need to enlarge on this, but in school we must make it felt that reports are very insignificant to us. We must spread this feeling throughout the school so that it becomes a kind of moral atmosphere.

You now have a picture of the school, because we have been through the whole range of subjects, with one exception; we still have to speak about how to incorporate technical subjects into school. We have not spoken of this yet, merely because there was no one there to do the work. I refer to needlework, which must still be included in some way. This must be considered, but until now there was no one who could do it. Of course it will also be necessary to consider the practical organization of the school; I must speak with you about who should teach the various classes, whether certain lessons should be given in the morning or afternoon, and so on. This must be discussed before we begin teaching. Tomorrow will be the opening festival, and then we will find time, either tomorrow or the day after, to discuss what remains concerning the practical distribution of work. We will have a final conference for this purpose where those most intimately concerned will be present. I shall then also have more to say about the opening ceremony.

## *Closing Words*

Today I would like to conclude these discussions by pointing out something I want to lay upon your hearts: that I would like you to stick firmly to the following four principles.

First, teachers must make sure that they influence and work on their pupils, in a broader sense, by allowing the spirit to flow through their whole being as teachers, and also in the details of their work: how each word is spoken, and how each concept or feeling is developed. Teachers must be people of initiative. They must be filled with initiative. Teachers must never be careless or lazy; they must, at every moment, stand in full consciousness of what they do in the school and how they act toward the children. This is the first principle. *The teacher must be a person of initiative in everything done, great and small.*

Second, my dear friends, we as teachers must take an interest in everything happening in the world and in whatever concerns humankind. All that is happening in the outside world and in human life must arouse our interest. It would be deplorable if we as teachers were to shut ourselves off from anything that might interest human beings. We should take an interest in the affairs of the outside world, and we should also be able to enter into anything, great or small, that concerns every single child in our care. That is the second principle. *The teacher should be one who is interested in the being of the whole world and of humanity.*

Third, *the teacher must be one who never compromises in the heart and mind with what is untrue.* The teacher must be true in the depths of being. Teachers must never compromise with untruth, because if they did, we would see how untruth would find its way through many channels into our teaching, especially in the way we present the subjects. Our teaching will only bear the stamp of truth when we ardently strive for truth in ourselves.

And now comes something more easily said than done, but it is, nevertheless, also a golden rule for the teacher's calling. *The teacher must never get stale or grow sour.* Cherish a mood of soul that is fresh and healthy! No getting stale and sour! This must be the teacher's endeavor.

And I know, my dear friends, that if during these two weeks you have properly received into your inner life what we were able to shed light on from the most diverse viewpoints, then indirectly, through the realms of feeling and will, what may still seem remote will come closer to your souls as you work with the children in the classroom. During these two weeks I have spoken only of what can enter directly into your practical teaching when you first allow it to work properly within your own souls. But our Waldorf school, my dear friends, will depend on what you do within yourselves, and whether you really allow the things we have considered to become effective in your own souls.

Think of the many things I have tried to clarify in order to come to a psychological view of the human being, especially of the growing human being. Remember these things. And maybe there will be moments when you feel unsure about how or when to bring one thing or another into your teaching, or where to introduce it, but if you remember properly what has been presented during these two weeks, then thoughts will surely arise in you that will tell you what to do. Of course many things should really be said many times, but I do not want to make you into teaching machines, but into free independent teachers. Everything spoken of during the past two weeks was given to you in this same spirit. The time has been so short that, for the rest, I must simply appeal to the understanding and devotion you will bring to your work.

Turn your thoughts again and again to all that has been said that can lead you to understand the human being, and especially the child. It will help you in all the many questions of method that may arise.

When you look back in memory to these discussions, then our thoughts will certainly meet again in all the various impulses that have come to life during this time. For myself, I can assure you that I will also be thinking back to these days, because right now this Waldorf school is indeed weighing heavily on the minds of those taking part in its beginning and organization. This Waldorf school must succeed; much depends on its success. Its success will bring a kind of proof of many things in the spiritual evolution of humankind that we must represent.

In conclusion, if you will allow me to speak personally for a moment, I would like to say: For me this Waldorf school will be a veritable child of concern. Again and again I will have to come back to this Waldorf school with anxious, caring thoughts. But when we keep in mind the deep seriousness of the situation, we can really work well together. Let us especially keep before us the thought, which will truly fill our hearts and minds, that connected with the present day spiritual movement are also the spiritual powers that guide the cosmos. When we believe in these good spiritual powers they will inspire our lives and we will truly be able to teach.

# First Lecture on the Curriculum

My dear friends, it would still be possible, of course, to present many more details from the field of general pedagogy. However, since we are always forced in such cases to conclude prematurely, we will use the remaining time this morning to take our general discussions of education over into an outline of instructional goals for the individual grades. In our general pedagogical studies, we have been trying to acquire the right point of view for dividing up the subject matter with regard to the development of the growing human being. We must always remember the necessity of consolidating our instruction in the way that I demonstrated. For example, we can proceed from mineralogy to geography or use ethnological characteristics to link history and geography when we deal with cultural history in a spiritual way. Bearing in mind this possibility of proceeding from one subject to another, let's go through the subject matter we want to present to our young charges and divide it into individual categories.

The first thing we need to consider when we welcome children into the first grade is to find appropriate stories to tell them and for them to tell back to us. In the telling and retelling of fairy tales, legends, and accounts of outer realities, we are cultivating the children's speech, forming a bridge between the local dialect and educated conversational speech. By making sure the children speak correctly, we are also laying a foundation for correct writing.

Parallel to such telling and retelling, we introduce the children to a certain visual language of forms. We have them draw simple round and angular shapes simply for the sake of the forms. As already mentioned, we do not do this for the sake of imitating some external object, but simply for the sake of the forms themselves. Also, we do not hesitate to link this drawing to simple painting, placing the colors next to each other so that the children get a feeling for what it means to place red next to green, next to yellow, and so on.

On the basis of what we achieve through this, we will be able to introduce the children to writing in the way that we have already considered from the perspective of educational theory. The natural way to go about it would be to make a gradual transition from form drawing to the Latin alphabet. Whenever we are in a position to introduce the Latin alphabet first, we should certainly do so, and then proceed from the Latin alphabet to German script. After the children have learned to read and write simple handwritten words, we make the transition to printed letters, taking the Latin alphabet first, of course, and following it up with the German.[1]

If we proceed rationally, we will get far enough in the first grade so that the children will be able to write simple things that we say to them or that they compose themselves. If we stick to simple things, the children will also be able to read them. Of course we don't need to aim at having the children achieve any degree of accomplishment in this first year. It would be completely wrong to expect that. The point is simply that, during the first grade, we should get the children to the

---

1. Steiner is referring here to the fact that the German language at that time was written in *Fraktur*, a specifically Germanic style of print and handwriting, rather than in the Latin, or Roman, alphabet now universally used for Western European languages. — TRANS.

point where they no longer confront the printed word as a total unknown, so to speak, and are able to take the initiative to write some simple things. This should be our goal with regard to language instruction, if I may put it like that.

We will be helped in this by what we are going to consider next—namely the elasticity and adaptability that the children's speech organs can gain from instruction in singing. Without our making a special point of it, they will develop a greater sensitivity to long and short vowels, voiced or voiceless sounds, and so on. Even though this may not be our intention in teaching music, the children will be introduced nonetheless to an auditory understanding of what the instrument of the voice produces in music—in a simple way at first, so that they can get ... well, of course it's impossible to get an over*view* of sounds, so I would actually have to invent a word and say: so that they can get an "over*hearing*" of it. By "over*hearing*" I mean that they really experience inwardly the single thing among the many, so that they are not overwhelmed by things as they perceive them.

In addition to this we must add something that can stimulate the children's thinking when we tell them about things that are close at hand, things that will later appear in a more structured form in geography and science. We explain such things and introduce them to the children's understanding by relating them to things that are already familiar—to familiar animals, plants, and soil formations, or to local mountains, creeks, or meadows. Schools call this "local history," but the purpose is to bring about a certain awakening in the children with regard to their surroundings; a soul awakening, so that they learn to really connect with their surroundings.

At the beginning of the second grade, we will continue with the telling and retelling of stories and try to develop this further. Then the children can be brought gradually to the point of writing down the stories we tell them. After they have had some practice in writing down what they hear, we can also have them write short descriptions of what we've told them about the animals, plants, meadows, and woods in the surroundings.

During the first grade it would be important not to touch on issues of grammar, and so on, to any great extent. In the second grade, however, we should teach the children the concepts of what a noun is, what an adjective is, and what a verb is. We should then connect this simply and graphically to a discussion of how sentences are constructed. With regard to descriptions, to thoughtfully describing their surroundings, we continue with what the children began in the first grade.

The third grade is essentially a continuation of the second with regard to speaking, reading, writing, and many other things. We will continue to increase the children's ability to write about what they see and read. Now we also try to summon up in them a conscious feeling for sounds that are short, long, drawn out, and so on. It is good to cultivate a feeling for articulating speech and for the general structure of language when the children are in third grade—that is, around the age of eight.[2] At this point, we attempt to convey an understanding of the different types of words and of the components and construction of a sentence—that is, of how punctuation marks such as commas and periods and so on are incorporated into a sentence.

Once again, with regard to telling and retelling, the fourth grade is a continuation of the third. When we take up short poems in the first and second grade, it's good to make a point of allowing the children to experience the rhythm, rhyme, and meter instinctively, and to wait to make them aware of the

---

2. The German translates literally as "in their eighth or ninth year" and is sometimes mistranslated in English as "eight or nine years old"; thus references to beginning school in "the seventh year" can be taken to mean that "children shouldn't go to school until they are seven." What Steiner said, however, was "in the seventh year of their life—that is, "six-going-on-seven." — TRANS.

poem's inner structure--that is, everything that relates to its inner beauty—until the third and fourth grades.

At that point, however, we try to lead everything the children have learned about writing descriptions and retelling stories in writing over into composing letters of all kinds. Then we try to awaken in the children a clear understanding of the tenses, of everything expressed by the various transformations of a verb. At around age nine, the children should acquire the concepts for what they need in this regard; they should get a feeling for it, so that they don't say "The man ran" when they should have said "The man has run"—that is, that they don't confuse the past tense with the present perfect. Children should get a feeling for when it is proper to say "He stood" rather than "He has stood," and other similar things that have to do with transformations in what a verb expresses. In the same way, we attempt to teach the children to feel instinctively the relationship between a preposition and its object. We should always make sure to help them get a feeling for when to use "on" instead of "at," and so on. Children who are going on ten should practice shaping their native language and should experience it as a malleable element.

In the fifth grade, it is important to review and expand on what we did in the fourth grade, and, from that point on, it is important to take into account the difference between active and passive verb forms. We also begin asking children of this particular age not only to reproduce freely what they have seen and heard, but also to quote what they have heard and read and to use quotation marks appropriately. We try to give the children a great deal of spoken practice in distinguishing between conveying their own opinions and conveying those of others. Through their writing assignments, we also try to arouse a keen distinction between what they themselves have thought, seen, and so forth, and what they communicate about what others have said. In this context, we again try to perfect their use of punctuation. Letter writing is also developed further.

In the sixth grade, of course we review and continue what we did in the fifth. In addition, we now try to give the children a strong feeling for the subjunctive mood. We use as many examples as possible in speaking about these things so that the children learn to distinguish between what can be stated as fact and what needs to be expressed in the subjunctive. When we have the children practice speaking, we make a special point of not allowing any mistakes in the use of the subjunctive, so that they assimilate a strong feeling for this inner dimension of the language. A child is supposed to say, "I am taking care that my little sister learn [subjunctive] how to walk," and not, "I am taking care that my little sister learns to walk."[3]

We now make the transition from personal letters to simple, concrete business compositions dealing with things the children have already learned about elsewhere. Even as early as the third grade we can extend what we say about the meadows and woods and so on to business relationships, so that later on the subject matter is already available for composing simple business letters.

In the seventh grade, we will again have to continue with what we did in the sixth grade, but now we also attempt to have the children develop an appropriate and flexible grasp of how to express wishing, astonishment, admiration, and so on in how they speak. We try to teach the children to form sentences in accordance with the inner configuration of these feelings. However, we do not need to mutilate poems or anything else in order to demonstrate how someone or other structured a sentence to express wishing. We approach it directly by having the children

---

3. These distinctions are not as readily detected in current English. In Steiner's example, the difference is between *lerne* and *lernt*; the first is perhaps closest to the process of learning (not yet fact), the second to having learned (fact).

themselves express wishes and shape their sentences accordingly. We then have them express admiration and form the sentences accordingly, or help them to construct the sentences. To further educate their ability to see the inner flexibility of language, we then compare their wishing sentences to their admiring ones.

What has been presented in science will already have enabled the children to compose simple characterizations of the wolf, the lion, or the bee, let's say. At this stage, alongside such exercises, which are directed more toward the universally human element in education, we must especially foster the children's ability to formulate practical matters of business. The teacher must be concerned with finding out about practical business matters and getting them into the student's heads in some sensible fashion.

In the eighth grade, it will be important to teach the children to have a coherent understanding of longer pieces of prose or poetry; thus, at this stage we will read a drama and an epic with the children, always keeping in mind what I said before: All the explanations and interpretations precede the actual reading of the piece, so that the reading is always the conclusion of what we do with the material. In particular, however, the practical business element in language instruction must not be disregarded in the eighth grade.

It will be important that we make it possible for children who have reached the fourth grade to choose to learn Latin. Meanwhile, we will have already introduced French and English [as foreign languages] in a very simple fashion as soon as the children have entered school.

When the children are in the fourth grade, we introduce them to Latin by having them listen to it, and we ask them to repeat little conversations as they gradually gain the ability to do so. We should certainly begin with speaking the language for the children to hear; in terms of speaking, we will attempt to achieve through listening what is usually accomplished in the first year of Latin instruction. We will then take this further according to the indications I gave in the lectures on educational theory, to the point where our eighth-grade graduates will have a mastery of Latin that corresponds to what is ordinarily taught in the fourth year of high school. In other words, our fourth graders must accomplish approximately what is usually taught in the first year of high school and our fifth and sixth graders what is usually taught in the second and third years respectively; the remainder of the time can be spent on what is usually taught in the fourth year.

Parallel to this we will continue with French and English [as foreign language] instruction, taking into account what we heard in the theoretical portion of these lectures.

We will also allow those who choose to study the Greek language to begin doing so. Here too, we proceed in the manner we heard about in the theoretical portion. Specifically, we attempt again to develop the writing of Greek letters on the basis of form drawing. It will be of great benefit to those who now choose to learn Greek to use a different set of letters to repeat the initial process of deriving writing from drawing.

Well, you have seen how we make free use of familiar things from the immediate surroundings for our independent instruction in general knowledge. In the third grade, when the children are going on nine, it is quite possible for this instruction to provide them with an idea of how mortar is mixed, for instance—I can only choose a few examples—and how it is used in building houses. They can also have an idea of how manuring and tilling are done, and of what rye and wheat look like. To put it briefly, in a very free way we allow the children to delve into the elements of their immediate surroundings that they are capable of understanding.

In the fourth grade we make the transition from this type of instruction to speaking about what belongs to recent history, still in a very free way. For example, we can tell the children how it happened that grapes came to be cultivated locally (if in fact that is the case), or how orchards were introduced or how one or the other industry appeared, and other similar things. Then, too, we draw on the geography of the local region, beginning with what is most readily available, as I have already described.

In the fifth grade, we make every effort to begin to introduce the children to real historical concepts. With fifth graders, we need not hesitate at all to teach the children about the cultures of Asian peoples and of the Greeks. Our fear of taking the children back into ancient times has occurred only because people in our day and age do not have the ability to develop concepts appropriate to these bygone times. However, if we constantly appeal to their feelings, it is easy enough to help ten- and eleven-year-olds develop an understanding of the Greeks and Asian peoples.

Parallel to this, as I showed you earlier, in geography we begin to teach the children also about soil formations and everything that is economically related to them, dealing first with the specific part of the Earth's surface that is most readily available.

Greek and Roman history and its aftereffects (until the beginning of the fifteenth century) belong to the sixth grade. In geography we continue with what we did in the fifth grade, taking a different part of the Earth and then linking its climatic conditions to astronomical conditions, examples of which we experienced yesterday afternoon.

In the seventh grade, it is important to get the children to understand how the modern life of humanity dawned in the fifteenth century, and we then describe the situation in Europe and so on up to about the beginning of the seventeenth century. This is one of the most important historical periods, and we must cover it with great care and attention. Indeed, it is even more important than the time immediately following it. In geography, we continue with the study of astronomical conditions and begin to cover the spiritual and cultural circumstances of Earth's inhabitants, of the various ethnic groups, but always in connection with what the children have already learned about material cultural circumstances—that is, economic circumstances—during their first two years of geography lessons.

In the eighth grade, we try to bring the children right up to the present in history, including a thorough consideration of cultural history. Most of what is included in history, as it is ordinarily taught, will only be mentioned in passing. It is much more important for children to experience how the steam engine, the mechanized loom, and so on have transformed the Earth than it is for them to learn at too young an age about such curiosities as the corrections made to the *Emser Depesche*.[4] The things our history books contain are the least important as far as the education of children is concerned. Even great figures in history, such as Charlemagne, should basically be covered only in passing. You will need to do a lot of what I told you yesterday about aids to guiding abstract concepts of time over into something concrete. Indeed, we must do a very great deal of it.

Now I probably do not need to tell you that even the subjects we have discussed so far will help the children develop an awareness of the spirit that permeates everything present in the world, an awareness that the spirit lives in our language, in the geographical elements covering the Earth, and in the flow of history. When we try to sense the living spirit in everything, we will also find the proper enthusiasm for conveying this living spirit to our students.

---

4. *Emser Depesche*: An incident that touched off the Franco-Prussian War of 1870. Bismark publicized an abridged and misleading version of a telegram (known as the "Ems Dispatch"), and the effect of this action was to feed the fury of the opposing parties in France and Prussia.

Whenever we do this, we will learn to compensate our students for what the religious denominations have been doing to humanity since the beginning of the modern era. These religious denominations, which have never made the free development of the individual a priority, have cultivated materialism from various angles. When it is not permissible to use the entire content of the world to teach people that the spirit is active, religious instruction becomes a breeding ground for materialism. The various religious denominations have made it their task to eliminate all mention of spirit and soul from any other form of instruction because they want to keep that privilege for themselves. Meanwhile the reality of these things has dried up as far as the religious denominations are concerned, and so what is presented in religious instruction consists merely of sentimental clichés and figures of speech. All the clichés that are now so terribly apparent everywhere are actually due more to religious culture than to international culture, because nowadays the emptiest clichés, which human instincts then carry over into outer life, are being promoted by the religious denominations. Certainly ordinary life also creates many clichés, but the greatest sinners in this respect are the religious denominations.

It remains to be seen, my dear friends, how religious instruction—which I will not even touch on in these discussions, because that will be the task of the congregations in question—will affect other types of instruction here in our Waldorf school. For now religious instruction is a space that must be left blank; these hours will simply be given over to the religion teachers to do whatever they choose. It goes without saying that they are not going to listen to us. They will listen to their church's constitution, or to their church gazette or that of the parochial school administration. We will fulfill our obligations in this respect, but we will also quietly continue to fulfill our obligation to summon up the spirit for our children in all the other subjects.

# Second Lecture on the Curriculum

STUTTGART, SEPTEMBER 6, 1919, A.M.

Now it's time to divide up the rest of the subjects and distribute them among the various grades.

It should be very clear that when the children are going on nine—that is, in the third grade—they should begin to study an appropriate selection of animals, which we must always relate to the human being, as in the example I presented to you.[1] This should be continued in the fourth grade, so that during the third and fourth grades we consider the animal kingdom scientifically in its relationship to the human being.

In the fifth grade, we begin to add less familiar animals. We also begin the study of botany as I described it in the theoretical portion of our seminar.[2] In the sixth grade, we continue with botany and begin the study of minerals, which should definitely be done in conjunction with geography.

In the seventh grade we return to the human being and attempt to teach what I pointed to yesterday with regard to what people need to learn about health and nutrition. We also attempt to apply the concepts the children have acquired in the fields of physics and chemistry to developing a comprehensive view of some specific commercial or industrial processes. All this should be developed out of science, in connection with what we are teaching in physics, chemistry, and geography.

---

1. See *Practical Advice to Teachers*, Rudolf Steiner Press, London, 1988, lecture 7.
2. See discussion 9, page 114.

In the eighth grade you will have to construct the human being by showing what is built in from the outside—the mechanics of the bones and muscles, the inner structure of the eye, and so on. Once again, you present a comprehensive picture of industrial and commercial relationships as they relate to physics, chemistry, and geography. If you build up your science lessons as we have just described, you will be able to make them incredibly lively and use them to awaken the children's interest in everything present in the world and in the human being.

Instruction in physics begins in the sixth grade and is linked to what the children have learned in music. We begin the study of physics by allowing acoustics to be born out of music. You should link acoustics to music theory and then go on to discuss the physiology of the human larynx from the viewpoint of physics. You cannot discuss the human eye yet, but you can discuss the larynx. Then, taking up only the most salient aspects, you go on to optics and thermodynamics. You should also introduce the basic concepts of electricity and magnetism now.

The following year, in the seventh grade, you expand on your studies of acoustics, thermodynamics, optics, electricity, and magnetism. Only then do you proceed to cover the most important basic concepts of mechanics—the lever, rollers, wheel and axle, pulleys, block and tackle, the inclined plane, the screw, and so on. After that you start from an everyday process such as combustion and try to make the transition to simple concepts of chemistry.

In the eighth grade you review and expand upon what was done in the seventh and then proceed to the study of hydraulics, of the forces that work through water. You cover everything belonging to hydraulics—water pressure, buoyancy, Archimedes' principle.

It would be great if we could stay here for three years giving lectures on education and providing examples of all the things you will have to figure out how to do yourselves out of your own inventiveness, but that can't be. We will have to be content with what has already been presented.

You conclude your study of physics, so to speak, with aerodynamics—that is, the mechanics of gases—discussing everything related to climatology, weather, and barometric pressure. You continue to develop simple concepts of chemistry so that the children also learn to grasp how industrial processes are related to chemical ones. In connection with chemical concepts, you also attempt to develop what needs to be said about the substances that build up organic bodies—starch, sugar, protein, and fat.

We must still apportion everything related to arithmetic, mathematics, and geometry and distribute it among the eight grades.

You know that standard superficial methodology dictates that in the first grade we should deal primarily with numbers up to 100. We can also go along with this, because the range of numbers doesn't really matter in the first grade, where we stick with simpler numbers. The main issue, regardless of what range of numbers you use, is to teach the arithmetical operations in a way that does justice to what I said before: Develop addition out of the sum, subtraction out of the remainder, multiplication out of the product and division out of the quotient—that is, exactly the opposite of how it's usually done. Only after you have demonstrated that 5 is 3 plus 2, do you demonstrate the reverse—that adding 2 and 3 yields 5. You must arouse in the children the powerful idea that 5 equals 3 plus 2, but that it also equals 4 plus 1, and so on. Thus, addition is the second step after separating the sum into parts, and subtraction is the second step after asking "What must I take away from a minuend to leave a specific difference?" and so on. As I said before, it goes without saying that you do this with simpler numbers in the first grade, but whether you chose a range of up to 95 or 100 or 105 is basically beside the point.

After that, however, when the second dentition is over, we can immediately begin to teach the children the times tables—even addition, as far as I'm concerned. The point is that children should memorize their times tables and addition facts as soon as possible after you have explained to them in principle what these actually mean—after you have explained this in principle using simple multiplication that you approach in the way we have discussed. That is, as soon as you've managed to teach the children the concept of multiplication, you can also expect them to learn the times tables by heart.

Then in the second grade you continue with the arithmetical operations using a greater range of numbers. You try to get the students to solve simple problems orally, in their heads, without any writing. You attempt to introduce unknown numbers by using concrete objects—I told you how you could approach unknown numbers using beans or whatever else is available. However, you should also not lose sight of doing arithmetic with known quantities.

In the third grade everything is continued with more complicated numbers, and the four arithmetical operations practiced during the second grade are applied to certain simple things in everyday life.

In the fourth grade we continue with what was done in the earlier grades, but we must now also make the transition to fractions and especially to decimal fractions.

In the fifth grade, we continue with fractions and decimals and present everything the children need to do independent calculations involving whole numbers, fractions, and decimals.

In the sixth grade we move on to calculating percentages, interest, discounts and the interest on promissory notes, which then forms the basis for algebra, as we have already seen.

I ask you to observe that, until the sixth grade, we have been deriving the geometric shapes—circle, triangle, and so on—from drawing, after having done drawing for the sake of writing in the first few years. Then we gradually made the transition from drawing done for the sake of writing to developing more complicated forms for their own sake—that is, for the sake of drawing, and also to do painting for the sake of painting. We guide instruction in drawing and painting into this area in the fourth grade, and in drawing we teach what a circle is, what an ellipse is, and so on. We develop this out of drawing. We continue this by moving on to three-dimensional forms, using plasticine if it's available, and whatever else you can get if it isn't—even if it's mud from the street, it doesn't matter! The point is to develop the ability to see and sense forms.

Mathematics instruction, geometry instruction, then picks up on what has been taught in this way in the drawing classes. Only then do we begin to explain in geometrical terms what a triangle, a square, or a circle is, and so on. That is, the children's spatial grasp of form develops through drawing. We begin to apply geometrical concepts to what they have learned in this way only once they are in the sixth grade. Then we have to make sure that we do something different in drawing.

In the seventh grade, after making the transition to algebra, we teach raising numbers to powers and extracting roots, and also what is known as calculating with positive and negative numbers. Above all, we try to introduce the children to what we might call practical, real-life applications of solving equations.

We continue this in the eighth grade and take the children as far as they can get with it. We also add calculating areas and volumes and the theory of geometrical loci, which we at least touched upon yesterday.

This gives you a picture of what you have to do with the children in mathematics and geometry.

As we have already seen, in the drawing lessons in the first few grades, we first teach the children to have a specific feeling for rounded or angular forms, and so on.

From these forms, we develop what we need for teaching writing. In these very elementary stages of teaching drawing, we avoid imitating anything. As much as possible, you should initially avoid allowing the children to copy a chair or a flower or anything else. As much as possible, you should have them produce linear forms—forms that are round, pointed, semicircular, elliptical, straight, and so on. Awaken in the children a feeling for the difference between the curve of a circle and the curve of an ellipse. In short, awaken their feeling for form before their urge to imitate wakes up! Wait until later before allowing them to apply what they have practiced in drawing forms to imitating actual objects. First have them draw angles so that they understand what an angle is through its shape. Then you show them a chair and say, "Look, here's an angle, and here's another angle," and so on. Do not let the children imitate anything until you have cultivated their feeling for independent forms which can be imitated later. Stick to this principle even when you move on to a more independent and creative treatment of drawing and painting.

Then in the sixth grade you introduce simple projection exercises and drawing shadows, both freehand and with a ruler and compass and the like. Make sure that the children have a good grasp of the concept and can reproduce in their drawings what the shadow of a sphere looks like on the surface of a cylinder if the cylinder is here and the sphere here and a light is shining on the sphere:

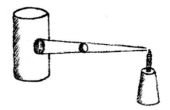

Yes, how shadows are cast! So a simple study of projection and shadows must take place in the sixth grade. The children must get a conception of it and must be able to imitate how more or less regular shapes or physical objects cast their shadows on flat and curved surfaces. In their sixth school year the children must acquire a concept of how the technical aspect unites with the element of beauty, of how a chair can be technically suited for a certain purpose while also having a beautiful form. The children must acquire both a concept and a hands-on grasp of this union of the technical and the beautiful.

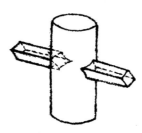

Then, in the seventh grade, everything having to do with one object penetrating another should be covered. As a simple example, you might say, "Here we have a cylinder with a post running through it. The post has to go through the cylinder." You must demonstrate what kind of a shape the post cuts in the surface of the cylinder when it enters and exits. This is something to learn together with the children. They must learn what happens when objects or surfaces interpenetrate, so that they know that it makes a difference whether a stovepipe goes

through the ceiling at a right angle, in which case their inter-
section is a circle, or at an angle, in which case it is an ellipse. In
addition, this is the year when the children must be taught a
good conception of perspective. So you do simple perspective
drawing with objects foreshortened in the distance and elon-
gated in the foreground, and you draw objects that are partially
concealed and so on. Once again, you combine the technical
aspect with beauty, so that you awaken in the children an idea
of whether or not it is beautiful when some portion of a wall of
a house is concealed by a projection, let's say. Some such pro-
jections are beautiful and others are not. These things have a
pronounced effect when they are taught to seventh graders in
particular—that is, to thirteen- or fourteen-year-olds.

In the eighth grade, all this is raised to an artistic level. All
the other subjects must be handled similarly to the ones we
have discussed. We will come back to this in the afternoon and
still add a few things to complete our curriculum. Above all, we
will have to see how music is developed in the first grade out of
elements that are as simple and elementary as possible, and
how from the third grade on the transition is made to more
complicated things. The point is that the children should be
able to take in those aspects of playing an instrument—especially of playing an instrument, but also of singing—that have
a creative and formative effect on their capabilities.

As special cases among all the other artistic subjects, we will
have to emphasize gymnastics and eurythmy, which must both
be developed out of the element of music and the other arts.

# Third Lecture on the Curriculum

STUTTGART, SEPTEMBER 6, 1919, P.M.

This morning it was pointed out that we can give only general guidelines for music, just as it is possible to give only general guidelines for the visual arts. The details, of course, must be left to the teacher's independent initiative. If you take these general guidelines in the right way, you will find that, basically, they are able to incorporate whatever you may find reasonable as musical instruction.

In the first, second, and third grades, we will essentially be dealing with very simple musical relationships, which should be applied with a view to developing the human voice and listening ability—that is, we should use the element of music to call upon the individual to use the human voice and the element of sound properly, and also to listen appropriately. I'm sure we all understand this.

Then come the fourth, fifth, and sixth grades. By then we will already be involved in explaining musical notation and will be able to do comprehensive scale exercises. Especially in the fifth and sixth grades, we will be able to go into the different keys and talk about D major and so on. We should wait as long as possible before introducing the minor keys, but by this point they too can be presented to the children.

However, the important thing now is to work from the opposite of our original point of view—that is, to get the children to adapt to the demands of music. This means leaning more toward the esthetic in our teaching. At first the children themselves were the focus, and we had to structure everything so that they would learn to listen and sing. But after having been encouraged in this during the first three grades, the children should then begin to adapt to the artistic demands of music, and the pedagogical element becomes the focus.

In the last two elementary grades—the seventh and eighth—I ask you to take into consideration the fact that the children must no longer have the feeling that they are being "trained" to do something, but must feel that they are making music for the pleasure it gives them, for the sake of enjoying it. This must be the thrust of our instruction in music. Therefore, during these two years the children's musical judgment can be awakened and educated. We can make them aware of the different character of different pieces of music, of the difference in character between a work by Beethoven and a work by Brahms. In simple ways, therefore, we should encourage the children to form opinions about music. Earlier, it was important to refrain from such opinions and judgments, but now we must cultivate them.

Now it will be especially important to understand one thing. You know I said something very similar this morning about the visual arts—that the way we initially use drawing allows writing to develop out of it. Later, however, drawing is used as an end in itself, and art itself becomes the important thing. As soon as the children progress from utilitarian forms of drawing and painting to developing independent artistic forms—in the third or fourth grade—it is also time to make the musical transition just described. At first we must work to affect the children physiologically; our work must help them adapt to the art of music. There should be a correspondence between these transitions in the graphic arts and in music.

One thing in the state curriculum is to our advantage—that there is no physical education instruction during the first three grades. So we may take the opportunity to begin with eurythmy. It would be very nice if eurythmy could be done in harmony with music instruction in the first grade, so that eurythmy would in fact help the children adapt to geometry and music. Not until the second grade would we begin to develop the gestures for the letters. This would be continued in the third grade, always linking eurythmy to music, geometry, and drawing.

Forms are added in the fourth, fifth, and sixth grades—for concrete and abstract expressions, and so on—since by now the children will have made enough progress in grammar to make this possible. This is continued in the seventh and eighth grades, but the forms become more complicated.

Starting in the fourth grade, this slot in the schedule is divided between eurythmy and physical education. In the fourth, fifth, and sixth grades, instruction in physical education should focus on the movement of the limbs and include everything that has to do with running, jumping, and climbing. Any exercises on gymnastic apparatus should be kept simple.

More complicated exercises involving equipment should not be done until the seventh and eighth grades. Meanwhile, the freeform exercises should be continued, and they should still all involve running, climbing, and jumping. If you go through all of what you've been able to conclude, I'm sure you will find that it agrees with the way I have tried to present this.

# Appendix

Discussion 5:
   Dass er dir log uns darf es nicht loben
   Nimm nicht Nonnen in nimmermüde Mühlen
   Rate mir mehrere Rätsel nur richtig

Discussion 6:
   Redlich ratsam
   Rüstet rühmlich
   Riesig rächend
   Ruhig Rollend
   Reuige Rosse

   Protzig preist
   Bäder brünstig
   Polternd putzig
   Bieder bastelnd
   Puder patzend
   Bergig brüstend

Discussion 7:
   Erfüllung geht
   Durch Hoffnung
   Geht durch Sehnen
   Durch Wollen
   Wollen weht
   Im Webenden
   Weht im Bebenden
   Webt bebend
   Webend bindend
   Im Finden
   Findend windend
   Kündend

Discussion 8:

In den unermesslich weiten Räumen,
In den endenlosen Zeiten,
In der Menschenseele Tiefen,
In der Weltenoffenbarung:
Suche des grossen Rätsels Lösung.

Protzig preist
Bäder brünstig
Polternd putzig
Bieder bastelnd
Puder patzend
Bergig Brüstend

Das er dir log, uns darf us nicht loben

Lalle Lieder lieblich
Lipplicher Laffe
Lappiger lumpiger
Leichiger Lurch.

Discussion 9:

Nimm mir nicht, was, wenn ich freiwillig dir es reiche,
dich beglückt.

Redlich ratsam
Rüstet rühmlich
Riesig rächend
Ruhig rollend
Reuige Rosse

Nimm nicht Nonnen in nimmermüde Mühlen

Pfiffig pfeifen
Pfäffische Pferde
Pflegend Pflüge
Pferchend Pfirsiche

Discussion 10:

Pfiffig pfeifen aus Näpfen
Pfäffische Pferde schlüpfend
Pflegend Pflüge hüpfend
Pferchend Pfirsiche Knüpfend

Kopfpfiffig pfeifen aus Näpfen
Napfpfäffische Pferde schlüpfend
Wipfend pflegend Pflüge hüpfend
Tipfend pferchend Pfirsiche Knüpfend

*Das Gebet* (from *Galgenlieder* by Christian Morgenstern)

Die Rehlein beten zur Nacht,
Hab acht!
Halb neun!
Halb zehn!
Halb elf!
Halb zwölf!
Zwölf!

Die Rehlein beten zur Nacht,
Hab acht!
Sie falten die kleinen Zehlein,
Die Rehlein

Discussion 11:

Ketzer petzten jetzt kläglich
Letztlich leicht skeptisch

Zuwider zwingen zwar
Zweizweckige Zwacker zu wenig
Zwanzig Zwerge,
Die sehnige Krebse
Sicher suchend schmausen,
Das schmatzende Schmachter
Schmiegsam schnellstens
Schnurrig schnalzen

(from *Wir fanden einen Pfad* by Christian Morgenstern)

Wer vom Ziel nichts weiss,
Kann den Weg nicht haben,
Wird im selben Kreis
All sein Leben traben;
Kommt am Ende hin
Wo er hergerückt,
Hat der Menge Sinn
Nur noch mehr zerstückt.

Discussion 12:

Ketzerkrächser petzten jetzt kläglich
Letzlich plötzlich leicht skeptisch

Nur renn nimmer reuig
Gierig grinsend
Knoten knipsend
Pfänder knüpfend

Discussion 13:

Klipp plack plick glick
Klingt Klapperrichtig
Knatternd trappend
Rossegetrippel

Discussion 15:

Schlinge Schlange geschwinde
Gewundene Fundewecken weg

Gewundene Fundewecken
Geschwinde schlinge schlange weg

Marsch schmachtender
Klappriger Racker
Krackle plappernd linkisch
Flink von vorne fort

Krackle plappernd linkisch
Flink von vorne fort
Marsch schmachtender
Klappriger Racker

# Further Reading

## Essential Works by Rudolf Steiner

*Anthroposophical Leading Thoughts: Anthroposophy as a Path of Knowledge: The Michael Mystery,* Rudolf Steiner Press, London, 1985.

*Anthroposophy (A Fragment),* Anthroposophic Press, Hudson, NY, 1996.

*An Autobiography,* Steinerbooks, Blauvelt, NY, 1977.

*Christianity as Mystical Fact,* Anthroposophic Press, Hudson, NY, 1997.

*The Foundation Stone / The Life, Nature, and Cultivation of Anthroposophy,* Rudolf Steiner Press, London, 1996.

*How to Know Higher Worlds: A Modern Path of Initiation,* Anthroposophic Press, Hudson, NY, 1994.

*Intuitive Thinking as a Spiritual Path: A Philosophy of Freedom,* Anthroposophic Press, Hudson, NY, 1995 (previously translated as *Philosophy of Spiritual Activity*).

*An Outline of Esoteric Science,* Anthroposophic Press, Hudson, NY, 1997 (previous translation titled *An Outline of Occult Science*).

*A Road to Self-Knowledge and The Threshold of the Spiritual World,* Rudolf Steiner Press, London, 1975.

*Theosophy: An Introduction to the Spiritual Processes in Human Life and in the Cosmos,* Anthroposophic Press, Hudson, NY, 1994.

## Books by Other Authors

Anschütz, Marieke. *Children and Their Temperaments,* Floris Books, Edinburgh, 1995.

Britz-Crecelius, Heidi. *Children at Play: Using Waldorf Principles to Foster Childhood Development,* Park Street Press, Rochester, VT,

1996.

Budd, Christopher Houghton (ed). *Rudolf Steiner, Economist: Articles & Essays*, New Economy Publications, Canterbury, UK, 1996.

Carlgren, Frans. *Education Towards Freedom: Rudolf Steiner Education: A Survey of the Work of Waldorf Schools Throughout the World*, Lanthorn Press, East Grinstead, England, 1993.

Childs, Gilbert. *Education and Beyond: Steiner and the Problems of Modern Society*, Floris Books, Edinburgh, 1996.

—— *Understanding Your Temperament! A Guide to the Four Temperaments*, Sophia Books, London, 1995.

Childs, Dr. Gilbert and Sylvia Childs. *Your Reincarnating Child*, Sophia Books/Rudolf Steiner Press, London, 1995.

Edmunds, L. Francis. *Renewing Education: Selected Writings on Steiner Education*, Hawthorn Press, Stroud, UK, 1992.

——*Rudolf Steiner Education: The Waldorf School*, Rudolf Steiner Press, London, 1992.

Fenner, Pamela Johnson and Karen L. Rivers, eds. *Waldorf Student Reading List*, third edition, Michaelmas Press, Amesbury, MA, 1995.

Finser, Torin M. *School as a Journey: The Eight-Year Odyssey of a Waldorf Teacher and His Class*, Anthroposophic Press, Hudson, NY, 1994.

Gabert, Erich. *Educating the Adolescent: Discipline or Freedom*, Anthroposophic Press, Hudson, NY, 1988.

Gardner, John Fentress. *Education in Search of the Spirit: Essays on American Education*, Anthroposophic Press, Hudson, NY, 1996.

——*Youth Longs to Know: Explorations of the Spirit in Education*, Anthroposophic Press, Hudson, NY, 1997.

Gatto, John Taylor. *Dumbing Us Down: The Hidden Curriculum of Compulsory Schooling*, New Society, Philadelphia, 1992.

Harwood, A. C. *The Recovery of Man in Childhood: A Study in the Educational Work of Rudolf Steiner*, The Myrin Institute of New York, New York, 1992.

Heider, Molly von. *Looking Forward: Games, rhymes and exercises to help children develop their learning abilities*, Hawthorn Press, Stroud, UK, 1995.

Heydebrand, Caroline von, *Childhood: A Study of the Growing Child*, Anthroposophic Press, Hudson, NY, 1995.

Jaffke, Freya. *Work and Play in Early Childhood*, Anthroposophic Press, Hudson, NY, 1996.

Large, Martin. *Who's Bringing Them Up? How to Break the T.V. Habit!* Hawthorn Press, Stroud, UK, 1990.

Logan, Arnold, ed. *A Garden of Songs for Singing and Piping at Home and School*, Windrose Publishing and Educational Services, Chatham, NY, 1996.

Maher, Stanford and Yvonne Bleach. *"Putting the Heart Back into Teaching": A Manual for Junior Primary Teachers*, Novalis Press, Cape Town, South Africa, 1996.

Maher, Stanford and Ralph Shepherd. *Standing on the Brink—An Education for the 21st Century: Essays on Waldorf Education*, Novalis Press, Cape Town, South Africa, 1995.

Nobel, Agnes. *Educating through Art: The Steiner School Approach*, Floris Books, Edinburgh, 1996.

Pusch, Ruth, ed. *Waldorf Schools Volume I: Kindergarten and Early Grades*, Mercury Press, Spring Valley, NY, 1993.

—— *Waldorf Schools Volume II: Upper Grades and High School*, Mercury Press, Spring Valley, NY, 1993.

Richards, M. C. *Opening Our Moral Eye*, Lindisfarne Books, Hudson, NY, 1996.

Spock, Marjorie. *Teaching as a Lively Art*, Anthroposophic Press, Hudson, NY, 1985.

# THE FOUNDATIONS
# OF WALDORF EDUCATION

THE FIRST FREE WALDORF SCHOOL opened its doors in
Stuttgart, Germany, in September, 1919, under the auspices of Emil
Molt, the Director of the Waldorf Astoria Cigarette Company and a student of Rudolf Steiner's spiritual science and particularly of Steiner's call
for social renewal.

It was only the previous year—amid the social chaos following the
end of World War I—that Emil Molt, responding to Steiner's prognosis
that truly human change would not be possible unless a sufficient number of people received an education that developed the whole human
being, decided to create a school for his workers' children. Conversations
with the minister of education and with Rudolf Steiner, in early 1919,
then led rapidly to the forming of the first school.

Since that time, more than six hundred schools have opened around
the globe—from Italy, France, Portugal, Spain, Holland, Belgium, Great
Britain, Norway, Finland, and Sweden to Russia, Georgia, Poland, Hun-
gary, Romania, Israel, South Africa, Australia, Brazil, Chile, Peru, Argen-
tina, Japan, and others—making the Waldorf school movement the
largest independent school movement in the world. The United States,
Canada, and Mexico alone now have more than 120 schools.

Although each Waldorf school is independent, and although there is
a healthy oral tradition going back to the first Waldorf teachers and to
Steiner himself, as well as a growing body of secondary literature, the
true foundations of the Waldorf method and spirit remain the many lectures that Rudolf Steiner gave on the subject. For five years (1919–24),
Rudolf Steiner, while simultaneously working on many other fronts,
tirelessly dedicated himself to the dissemination of the idea of Waldorf
education. He gave manifold lectures to teachers, parents, the general
public, and even the children themselves. New schools were founded.
The movement grew.

While many of Steiner's foundational lectures have been translated
and published in the past, some have never appeared in English, and
many have been virtually unobtainable for years. To remedy this situation and to establish a coherent basis for Waldorf education, Anthroposophic Press has decided to publish the complete series of Steiner lectures
and writings on education in a uniform series. This series will thus con-
stitute an authoritative foundation for work in educational renewal, for
Waldorf teachers, parents, and educators generally.

## RUDOLF STEINER'S LECTURES (AND WRITINGS) ON EDUCATION

I. *Allgemeine Menschenkunde als Grundlage der Pädagogik. Pädagogischer Grundkurs,* 14 Lectures, Stuttgart, 1919 (GA 293). Previously *Study of Man.* **The Foundations of Human Experience** (Anthroposophic Press, 1996).

II. *Erziehungskunst Methodische-Didaktisches,* 14 Lectures, Stuttgart, 1919 (GA 294). **Practical Advice to Teachers** (Anthroposophic Press, 2000).

III. *Erziehungskunst,* 15 Discussions, Stuttgart, 1919 (GA 295). **Discussions with Teachers** (Anthroposophic Press, 1997).

IV. *Die Erziehungsfrage als soziale Frage,* 6 Lectures, Dornach, 1919 (GA 296). **Education as a Force for Social Change** (previously *Education as a Social Problem*) (Anthroposophic Press, 1997).

V. *Die Waldorf Schule und ihr Geist,* 6 Lectures, Stuttgart and Basel, 1919 (GA 297). **The Spirit of the Waldorf School** (Anthroposophic Press, 1995).

VI. *Rudolf Steiner in der Waldorfschule, Vorträge und Ansprachen,* Stuttgart, 1919–1924 (GA 298). **Rudolf Steiner in the Waldorf School—Lectures and Conversations** (Anthroposophic Press, 1996).

VII. *Geisteswissenschaftliche Sprachbetrachtungen,* 6 Lectures, Stuttgart, 1919 (GA 299). **The Genius of Language** (Anthroposophic Press, 1995).

VIII. *Konferenzen mit den Lehren der Freien Waldorfschule 1919–1924,* 3 Volumes (GA 300). **Faculty Meetings with Rudolf Steiner,** 2 volumes (Anthroposophic Press, 1998).

IX. *Die Erneuerung der Pädagogisch-didaktischen Kunst durch Geisteswissenschaft,* 14 Lectures, Basel, 1920 (GA 301). **The Renewal of Education** (Anthroposophic Press, 2001).

X. *Menschenerkenntnis und Unterrichtsgestaltung,* 8 Lectures, Stuttgart, 1921 (GA 302). Previously *The Supplementary Course—Upper School* and *Waldorf Education for Adolescence.* **Education for Adolescents** (Anthroposophic Press, 1996).

XI. *Erziehung und Unterrricht aus Menschenerkenntnis,* 9 Lectures, Stuttgart, 1920, 1922, 1923 (GA 302a). The first four lectures available as **Balance in Teaching** (Mercury Press, 1982); last three lectures as **Deeper Insights into Education** (Anthroposophic Press, 1988).

XII. *Die Gesunder Entwicklung des Menschenwesens,* 16 Lectures, Dornach, 1921–22 (GA 303). **Soul Economy: Body, Soul, and Spirit in Waldorf Education** (Anthroposophic Press, 2003).

XIII. *Erziehungs- und Unterrichtsmethoden auf Anthroposophischer Grundlage,* 9 Public Lectures, various cities, 1921–22 (GA 304). **Waldorf Education and Anthroposophy 1** (Anthroposophic Press, 1995).

XIV. *Anthroposophische Menschenkunde und Pädagogik,* 9 Public Lectures, various cities, 1923–24 (GA 304a). ***Waldorf Education and Anthroposophy 2*** (Anthroposophic Press, 1996).

XV. *Die geistig-seelischen Grundkräfte der Erziehungskunst,* 12 Lectures, 1 Special Lecture, Oxford 1922 (GA 305). ***The Spiritual Ground of Education*** (Anthroposophic Press, 2004).

XVI. *Die pädagogisch Praxis vom Gesichtspunkte geisteswissenschaftlicher Menschenerkenntnis,* 8 Lectures, Dornach, 1923 (GA 306). ***The Child's Changing Consciousness As the Basis of Pedagogical Practice*** (Anthroposophic Press, 1996).

XVII. *Gegenwärtiges Geistesleben und Erziehung,* 4 Lectures, Ilkeley, 1923 (GA 307). ***A Modern Art of Education*** (Anthroposophic Press Press, 2004) and ***Education and Modern Spiritual Life*** (Garber Publications, n.d.).

XVIII. *Die Methodik des Lehrens und die Lebensbedingungen des Erziehens,* 5 Lectures, Stuttgart, 1924 (GA 308). ***The Essentials of Education*** (Anthroposophic Press, 1997).

XIX. *Anthroposophische Pädagogik und ihre Voraussetzungen,* 5 Lectures, Bern, 1924 (GA 309). ***The Roots of Education*** (Anthroposophic Press, 1997).

XX. *Der pädagogische Wert der Menschenerkenntnis und der Kulturwert der Pädagogik,* 10 Public Lectures, Arnheim, 1924 (GA 310). ***Human Values in Education*** (Anthroposophic Press, 2005).

XXI. *Die Kunst des Erziehens aus dem Erfassen der Menschenwesenheit,* 7 Lectures, Torquay, 1924 (GA 311). ***The Kingdom of Childhood*** (Anthroposophic Press, 1995).

XXII. *Geisteswissenschaftliche Impulse zur Entwicklung der Physik. Erster naturwissenschaftliche Kurs: Licht, Farbe, Ton—Masse, Elektrizität, Magnetismus,* 10 Lectures, Stuttgart, 1919–20 (GA 320). ***The Light Course*** (Anthroposophic Press, 2001).

XXIII. *Geisteswissenschaftliche Impulse zur Entwicklung der Physik. Zweiter naturwissenschaftliche Kurs: die Wärme auf der Grenze positiver und negativer Materialität,* 14 Lectures, Stuttgart, 1920 (GA 321). ***The Warmth Course*** (Mercury Press, 1988).

XXIV. *Das Verhältnis der verschiedenen naturwissenschaftlichen Gebiete zur Astronomie. Dritter naturwissenschaftliche Kurs: Himmelskunde in Beziehung zum Menschen und zur Menschenkunde,* 18 Lectures, Stuttgart, 1921 (GA 323). Available in typescript only as **"The Relation of the Diverse Branches of Natural Science to Astronomy."**

XXV. ***The Education of the Child and Early Lectures on Education*** (A collection) (Anthroposophic Press, 1996).

XXVI. Miscellaneous.

# Index

Demosthenes, 59
dialect, 53, 183
diet
  affect on learning capacity,
    102-105, 107, 110-111
  stimulants, 110-111
  temperamental individuation of,
    32
  *See also* food; health and nutrition
digestion, 103, 105
disposition of child, 13
  *See also* temperament
drawing lessons, 26, 27, 36, 42-43,
    52-53, 176, 199-200, 203-204
  to enhance learning, 51, 107, 112,
    148-149, 167, 184, 190, 198-
    199
  *See also* art; mental images;
    painting
dreams, 129
Dühring, Karl Eugen, 160-161

E
Earth
  movement in space, 156
  and plants, 115-121, 124-
    125, 128-131, 137, 143-144
  sleeping and waking of, 125, 128-
    129, 131-133, 138
  teaching about, 148, 191-
    192
education
  spiritual requirements for, 20
  to complete human being,
    14
  *See also* teacher; teaching
egoism, 60, 79
Egyptian culture, 169-170
electricity, 64, 110, 195
*Emser Depesche*, 192
English
  language, 189-190
  spirit, 64
  *See also* language
etheric body

as component of human being, 14
  manifestation of according to
    temperament, 14, 33
  mother-principle affecting, 61
  relation to astral body, 62
Europe, 191
  Crusades affecting, 88-93
  Magyar invasions, 162-164
  *See also* history
eurythmy, 23, 26, 80, 105-106,
    108-110, 201, 204
  *See also* gymnastics; movement
evolution
  instruction about, 85, 94-95
  of state, 174
examinations
  effect of on child, 25-26
experience, temperamental quality
    of, 38
eye, 195

F
fables
  The Does Prayer, 127
  The Nightingale and the Peacock,
    70
  The Oak, 100-101
  The Sheepdog, 74
  The Souls' Awakening, 62
  The Steed and the Bull, 82
  We Found a Path, 136
  *See also* poetry; story-telling
fairy tales
  use in lesson presentation,
    22, 23, 36, 54, 69
  *See also* story-telling
Fallersleben, Hofmann von, 77
father-principle, 61-62
feelings
  cultivation of, 70-71, 118,
    124, 128, 134, 161-162, 191
  diversion of, 96-97
  effect on of teaching, 26, 45,
    67
  as guide to lesson presenta-

CPSIA information can be obtained
at www.ICGtesting.com
Printed in the USA
FFOW05n0518280617